The Thirties and the War Years

The Thirties and the War Years

Anton Rippon

First published in Great Britain in 2014 by

North Bridge Publishing
20 Chain Lane
Mickleover
Derby DE3 9AJ

ISBN 978-0-9926779-5-4

Book design by Graham Hales, Derby
Printed and bound by 4Edge Ltd, Essex

Contents

Introduction

THERE can have been few more significant decades for Derby than the 1930s and 1940s. As Britain mainly struggled through the effects of the Great Depression that had started in the United States and – like the bad weather that America so often sends us – had blown across the Atlantic to affect life here in the '30s, the market and industrial town of Derby suffered less than most.

While elsewhere businesses struggled, Derby bucked the trend and even prospered. As much of the United Kingdom wondered where the next decent meal might come from, Derby rebuilt its town centre. In the 1930s new civic buildings and an imaginatively designed bus station sprang up here. We still enjoy much of it today (although not the bus station, of course).

It could have been different, though. In 1942, Alderman Will Raynes told the *Derby Evening Telegraph*: "I would like to stand on The Spot and, looking down St Peter's Street, get a clear and unimpeded view of the beautiful tower of Derby Cathedral."

He was talking about his plan to demolish the entire town centre and replace it with an industrial area. If Raynes had had his way, almost every building from The Spot to the Cathedral would have been razed to the ground to make way for a 150ft-wide road lined by seven-storey blocks. There would have been elevated roadways along the entire length of Albert Street, over part of Victoria Street and into Green Lane, and over East Street and St Peter's Churchyard.

Horrible thought, isn't it? But, at various times in Derby's modern story, any of these might have come about. Indeed, the idea to flatten the old town centre and replace shops and houses with industrial units had first been floated just after the First World War. Happily, none if it ever came to pass, but the next time we complain about what Derby's planners have done to our city let us remember – it could have been worse.

Of course, by the time that Alderman Raynes was unveiling his thoughts, Derby was engulfed in another world war. The 1930s, that had proved so positive for the town, had ended in a darkness the like of which the world had never before seen. Derby stepped up magnificently to the challenge of the Second World War. Its men and women gave of their best; its industry was vital to the eventual victory over Nazism.

This book attempts – through events great and small, many of them reported in the *Derby Evening Telegraph* – to paint a picture of what it was like to live in Derby between 1930 and 1945. There was a never a time like it before, and there has never been a time like it since.

Anton Rippon
Derby
2014

Derby in the Thirties

1930

A record day for holidaymakers

HOLIDAY traffic in Derby broke all records in the glorious June of 1930. On Whit Weekend alone, day-trippers were setting off in the early hours of the morning. The first holiday special train left Friargate Station at 4.15am, bound for Scarborough and laden with 500 passengers. From Friargate, duplicate services were run to Skegness, while the crowds at the LMS Station were so great that the railway companies had to bring in extra platform staff to control the crush.

The Trent Motor Traction Company dealt with the heaviest Whitsun demand it had ever known, and every available omnibus was put on the road.

Those who decided to stay in the town added to the crush. No fewer than 67,000 people used Derby's tramcars and buses – a record for a Sunday. Over 10,000 Derbeians took advantage of the newly opened Darley Abbey Park, where hundreds of families picnicked beside the River Derwent and wandered among the beautiful gardens. Thousands more listened to the band of the Coldstream Guards at Derby Arboretum, which was lit by fairy lights and floodlight beams until 10.30pm. Several hundred went to Victoria Park, Ilkeston, to hear the Stanton Ironworks Band, while at Alfreton Park, the Swanwick Colliery Silver Band entertained hundreds more who also enjoyed the rhododendrons that were at their absolute best. The owner of Alfreton Hall, Mr Palmer-Morewood, annually opened his park to the townsfolk.

But amidst all the fun, there was also tragedy. Sixteen-year-old Lawrence Nolan of Oxford Street, Derby, was killed when his bicycle was in collision with a car driven by Ernest Hunt, a Ripley newsagent.

The accident happened at Little Eaton, where young Lawrence and a friend had planned to camp for the weekend. One of a family of seven children, he had just started work in the parcels office of Ranby's store in Victoria Street.

A tragic romance that began in Derby

A TRAGIC romance of unrequited love that began in Derby was revealed at the inquest of an artists' model in December 1930.

Two years earlier, while working on a five-week engagement at Derby Art School, 25-year-old Molly Chaddock had been introduced to an actor, Charles Callum, at the theatrical boarding house where they were both staying in the town. Callum was appearing at the Grand Theatre in Babington Lane, in a production of *The Wrecker* by Arnold Ridley (who later found new fame as Private Godfrey in *Dad's Army*).

A London inquest heard that Miss Chaddock had fallen in love with Callum, but upon hearing of his marriage, in America, to another artists' model – a beautiful Russian – she had committed suicide by putting her head in the gas oven at her parents' Fulham home.

Her mother told the inquest: "Derby was an entirely strange town to my daughter, but I liked it very much from visits I had made to a distant relative of mine, Mr Turner of Mill Hill Lane. I was always careful about lodgings for my daughter, and I wrote to Mr Turner and asked him to send me a local paper and for advice on lodgings. Although we did not know it at the time, the lodgings selected were used mainly by theatrical touring parties."

It was here that she met Callum, and although he was 12 years her senior, she fell head over heels in love with him. Her mother continued: "The friendship continued when they returned to London, but it was evident that he did not have the same regard for her as she had for him." Charles Callum went to America, while Molly Chaddock entered hospital for an operation. She was recuperating when she learned that he had married Manya Gaines in New York. Her father, Major Harry Chaddock, told the inquest: "'Charles has married,' she cried, and she sobbed for hours. My wife tried to comfort her and at 3am we thought she was asleep. But in the morning my wife smelled gas and found her lying on the floor, her head resting on cushions in the oven, the taps full on."

Molly Chaddock, the girl whose visit to Derby had ultimately led to her tragic death, was a niece of Captain Matthew Webb, the first man to swim the English Channel.

Derby's sorrow at airship disaster

ON Sunday, 5 October 1930, the *Derby Daily Telegraph* called staff into its new offices at the old Corn Exchange in Albert Street, to work on the production of a special edition. In the early hours of that morning the R101 airship, Britain's pride, had crashed into a hillside near Beauvais in northern France, during a storm.

For many Derbeians, it was almost a personal tragedy. Messrs Haslam and Newton had made the airship's electrical controls at their Derby works, and on 18 October 1929, the giant airship had flown over the town during its second trial flight from Cardington in Bedfordshire. It was a sight that brought thousands of people on to the streets and traffic to a standstill. Another trial flight, on which Derby's former mayor, William Raynes, was due to be a passenger, had been cancelled because of bad weather.

Among the 48 passengers who perished on the maiden flight, which was bound for India, was Lord Thomson of Cardington, the

Air Minster. During the 1924 General Election campaign, Lord Thomson had spoken at the Central Hall, Derby, in support of the town's Labour MP, Jimmy Thomas. Also killed was Sir Sefton Brancker, the Director of Civil Aviation. As president of the newly formed Derby Aero Club, he had recently attended the club's dinner at the Midland Hotel.

The photograph of the burnt-out airship that appeared on the front page of that *Telegraph* Sunday special edition was taken by a British photographer, who was flown to France and then back to Croydon. A print was rushed to St Pancras and put on a Derby-bound train, arriving in the town at 6.11pm. The emergency edition, complete with photograph, was on sale well before 7pm, the *Telegraph* claiming that it was the only newspaper in the Midlands to carry a picture of the disaster. Considering the technology of the times, it was certainly a remarkable achievement to be on the streets so soon after receiving the image.

Bad news for Derby's Hippodrome

IN February 1930, the manager of Derby Hippodrome in Green Lane had some bad news for his patrons. Ernest Vincent normally knew what shows were due to be playing at his theatre up to 12 months ahead. But now the cinema was affecting theatre audiences nationwide.

"I can't tell you what we are showing even two months ahead," said Vincent. "The talkies have scared theatre producers," he explained.

On 14 June that year, live theatre ceased at the Hippodrome. And working on the theory that, if you can't beat them, then join them, on 15 September, the venue reopened as a cinema. With 1,000 new tip-up seats in the stalls, the Hippodrome was showing the new 20th Century Fox musical comedy film *Sunny Side Up*, starring Janet Gaynor and Charles Farrell and featuring the song, *If I Had a Talking Picture Of You*. It was the start of 20-year career as a cinema for the Hippodrome, before it became a theatre again.

Derby Hippodrome pictured after the former theatre had given in to the advancing tide of the cinema.

Less than ten years after its conversion to a cinema, the Hippodrome enjoyed its greatest moment when Anna Neagle, star of the colour film, *Sixty Glorious Years* in which she played Queen Victoria, made a personal appearance there when the film was screened. That night, Miss Neagle slept at the Midland Hotel, in the same room that Queen Victoria herself had occupied when she visited Derby in 1849.

In December 1930, the *Derby Daily Telegraph* carried advertisements for just seven cinemas. The White Hall – later to become the Odeon – in St Peter's Street was showing *Song of the Flame*, a musical based on the 1925 operetta by Oscar Hammerstein II. Lon Chaney's first talkie, *Unholy Three* was on at the Cosy in London Road, while another Chaney film, *Thunder*, could be seen at the Alexandra on Normanton Road. The Normanton showed *White Cargo*, while back in the town centre, *Court Scandal* was on at the Picture House in Babington Lane, and *Puttin' on the Ritz* at the Empire, later the Black Prince, in Colyear Street. That year's panto was a Randolph Sutton production of *Cinderella* at the Grand Theatre in Babington Lane.

Derby's Art Deco Bus Station, newly built in May 1933.

Marks and Spencer – but no airport

IN 1930, the new Marks and Spencer building rose up at the bottom of St Peter's Street. Designed by Robert Lutyens, the son of Edwin Lutyens who designed the Cenotaph in Whitehall, the M&S Derby store was described as "of the Modern movement with art deco and neo-classical motifs in Portland Stone masonry."

The 1930s also saw the redevelopment of Derby's river bank: the Central Improvement Plan that eventually incorporated the Bus Station, Council House, Police Station and Magistrates' Court. The redevelopment got under way with the building of a new Exeter Bridge and in 1930 the *Derby Daily Telegraph* carried several pictures as the work progressed. One image showed a giant drill at work on the site of the new bridge. The caption writer asked: "Does your dentist use one of these?"

The future of one development did look decidedly shaky, however. In 1930, Derby Corporation's Derby Aerodrome Sub Committee announced that both the sites they had earlier identified as possibilities were now non-starters. The sub committee suddenly decided that their Radbourne site was, after all, "out of the way",

Public transport dominates St Peter's Street. The newly opened Marks & Spencer store can be seen on the left.

while the Boulton site might now be needed "for a line for the proposed 'grid' electricity system for Alvaston". Of course, Derby Airport was opened at Burnaston before the Second World War, but it is fascinating to think that local holidaymakers could have been flying out of Radbourne or Boulton.

1931

Hands up – it's carnival time!

ANYONE walking down the Wardwick one particularly warm July Saturday in 1931 was likely to be accosted by a one-eyed ruffian who demanded money. Elsewhere in the town centre, a spate of bank robberies was reported, but, according to the *Derby Daily Telegraph*, the local CID simply wished the perpetrators: "Good hunting."

Motorists who failed to hand over cash were "gingered up" at the point of a revolver. One 6ft-tall brigand raided Northcliffe House in Albert Street, striding through the *Telegraph* offices with a drawn sword after announcing his arrival with a bugle call. In St Peter's Street, the vicar of Boulton St Mary's, Rev J. F. Young, was taken prisoner and held to ransom. It was not, however, a case of your worst nightmare coming true, simply the high jinks involved in the annual Derby Hospital Day carnival.

"There is every indication that 1931 is going to be a record year," Mr J. P. Hudson, secretary of the collecting committee, told the *Telegraph*.

"Eight hundred collecting boxes are out, apart from the flag sellers. 'The Man With The Gun' returned two boxes filled before noon. Last year he collected between £7 and £8 and this year he is hoping to get £10."

Today, it is hard to imagine that such fund raising activities would be allowed. Armed police would be the most likely response. But over 80 years ago, Derbeians had no such concerns. Just in case anyone was concerned, however, the *Telegraph* pointed out that official collectors, whether in fancy dress or not, were wearing green rosettes and carrying boxes marked with the official Hospital Day label. Derby Toc H collectors were dressed as "Good Night" or "Nightmare" to warn everybody of unhappy sleep that night unless they gave generously.

Derby's householders received their bread and groceries in specially decorated vehicles that local tradesmen had prepared specially for the carnival, and there were eight bands in the carnival parade itself, including those of the Sherwood Foresters, Derby Town Prize Band, Cordon Street Mission Silver Band and the Davenport Wesleyan Silver Band.

It was also a special day for the town's horses. Freshly groomed, with their hooves and harness shining, 43 horses, with carts attached, formed up in the Cattle Market for their own parade to the Arboretum where judging would take place. It was the Derby Co-operative Society's entry – a milk float drawn by a smart cob – that caught most people's eyes.

Streets along the parade route were decorated with flags and bunting, and in the carnival procession itself, Judy's Hospital Workers has four tableaux: Alice in Wonderland; A Fairyland Wedding; Dolly Blues; and Policemen. There were also decorated fire engines and tramcars, and floats from many Derby shops and factories, churches and chapels.

By the time the Queen of the Carnival was crowned in the Market Place that afternoon, a shower of rain threatened to spoil the ceremony. But no-one's spirits were dampened as the Mayor, Councillor Harold Hoare, placed the crown on the head of Miss Phyllis Murdock, a member of the DRI staff, radiant in a period gown. The Mayor gave her a silver wristwatch, while her six maids of honour each received Oriental necklaces. And then Derby's annual fun day was over for another year.

Great reception for a famous boxer

THE frail looking Welshman from Pontypridd may have left his boxing days behind him, but when former world flyweight champion, Jimmy Wilde, refereed at Derby Drill Hall in Becket Street in October 1931, a bumper crowd turned out to see him. A former boxing booth fighter, Wilde had been a phenomenal puncher, despite weighing only about seven stones. In 1916, he had earned the right to call himself world champion after beating Plymouth's Joe Symonds. But the Americans, who later that year sent over their champion, Young Zulu Kid, had disputed the world title. Wilde had settled the matter once and for all by knocking out Young Zulu Kid at Holborn's Central Hall.

Wilde's left hook earned him the nickname of "the Ghost With a Hammer in His Hand," but he was way past his best in June 1923, when he lost his world title to Pancho Villa, and never fought again.

But it was not the last that boxing would see of Wilde, and at Derby that Wednesday evening in 1931 he brought the house down.

The *Derby Daily Telegraph* reported: "What an amazing hold little Jimmy Wilde still has on the army of British boxing enthusiasts. A huge crowd at the Drill Hall last night cheered themselves hoarse as the Welsh wizard climbed through the ropes ... Of the great audience, fully half had been attracted by Jimmy.

"The 5th (Territorial) Battalion of the Sherwood Foresters, who arranged the show, did a good stroke of business when they put that world-famed name on the programme. Anyone less like an ex-world champion it is difficult to imagine. A mild little man with a broad, slow smile, he looks as though he were just 'a man in the street' rather than the finest flyweight in history.

"He was cheered when he got into the ring. He was cheered when he got out. He was cheered when he spoke, and the crowd screamed frenzied approval when he put a ban on smoking. Mind you, only Jimmy could do this. Anyone else would have been cheerfully ignored, but Wilde has personality and a way of getting what he wants.

"After given his decision in the big fight, a few lone spirits started to hoot. Like a prairie fire it spread until the hoots outnumbered the more self-contained.

"Then Jimmy stepped forward: 'What's the matter?" he said, "What are you hooting for? You don't know anything about boxing.'

That was enough. Someone started to cheer, and within a minute all those who had been manfully booing were howling: 'Good old Jimmy.'"

Councillors' "luxuries" called to account

WHEN Derby's elective auditors published their annual report in December 1931, their one headline-grabbing recommendation was that local councillors and officials should cut down on their expenses when attending conferences – and that official visits to France should be discontinued altogether.

They singled out a visit to France by the Town Clerk and two aldermen, saying that while the £62 cost was not a comparatively large amount, "it is a luxury we can well do without".

And while the personal expenses of those attending conferences had been made in accordance with the approved scale, the auditors observed: "The total cost is a truly heavy figure, and we trust that the responsible officers will do everything possible to curtail such expenditure."

They felt that visits to conferences and the number of Derby representatives could be reduced significantly without in any way impairing the efficiency of the Corporation. Also coming in for criticism was the money spent on the opening ceremony of the new Exeter Bridge, where more than £46 had been spent on wine, cigars, car hire and the printing of menus.

It also appeared that many of Derby's council house tenants were not too keen to pay their rents. "Assuming that a large proportion of arrears in Corporation rentals are irrecoverable, the total of £1,984 13s 8d written off during the last 12 months still appeared to be somewhat heavy."

The role of the Derby Borough Development Committee – designed to bring new business to the town – was also called into question. Indeed, the auditors felt that it ought to be wound up altogether.

"We submit that the committee has outlived its period of usefulness." The Development Committee had cost ratepayers nearly £450 in the previous 12 months, all but £100 of that going on secretarial expenses. "It is not a fair proposition from the point of view of the ratepayers," said the auditors.

Prince George opens Derby's new "lungs"

THOUSANDS of local schoolchildren were given some royal advice at Darley Park on a beautiful July day in 1931, when 29-year-old Prince George, the fourth son of King George V, told them to safeguard what had just been handed to them. The prince had just formally opened the park – and another at Markeaton – and warned the children not to let "the exuberance of youth lead to any destructiveness or untidiness" and that they should look upon both parks as their own possessions.

So far as the provision of "lungs" for the town was concerned the early 1930s were important years for Derby. The town had complied with the Town Planning Act by having 10 per cent of its total acreage as open spaces. Indeed, Derby now had more than 500 acres of parks and open spaces, comparable, it seemed, to any town or city in the land. "All Derby wants now is an aerodrome," said the Mayor, Councillor Harold Hoare.

For centuries the grounds at Markeaton had been the property of the Mundy family. Now, and for the next few months, workman would be engaged in clearing up the grounds, laying flower beds and gravel paths, and generally turning what had grown into a wilderness into a neat, modern park. The land surrounding the mansion would be transformed into a pleasure garden with flowerbeds and ornamental masonry work. Markeaton stream, as the *Telegraph* called it, which ran through the park, would be widened to provide a boating lake, half a mile long and between 20 to 80 yards wide.

Darley Park – or Darley Abbey Park to give it is proper title – with its Darley Hall, had fallen into the council's hands following the death of Mrs Ada Evans in 1929. Within a very short space of time, the town of Derby had been gifted two large and very beautiful parks. Darley, in particular, with its wonderful riverside aspect, was a jewel. Now a royal prince had come to declare them officially open to all Derbeians. The prince planted a commemorative tree at Markeaton Park. On his way from a decorated grandstand, from which he had made his speech, to Darley Hall, where he would take tea, the royal visitor paused to plant another tree.

He told the crowd: "Darley Abbey and these grounds have been well laid out and will, no doubt, become one of your chief open-air attractions. Parks have often been termed the lungs of a town and I am sure that the money spent on them must be a good investment. Without them, the health of the town must suffer."

Sir John Ferguson Bell told the crowd: "The Corporation has been very much assisted by the generosity of the former owners of these parks. Markeaton Park belonged to the Mundy family, and the Rev Clark-Maxwell, the heir, approached me when I was mayor and offered to let us have the Georgian house, and the Italian gardens and the park at very much below their value. If he had been a rich man he would have presented the house and park to the town."

1932

Derby awash in the great flood

ON 22 May 1932, residents in the Brook Street area of Derby were awakened by the sound of water rushing through their downstairs rooms. The latest version of the Great Derby Flood was upon the town.

Shortly after 5.30am on that Sunday morning over 80 years ago, Markeaton Brook, so often the cause of serious flooding down the ages, burst its banks to leave the centre of Derby under several feet of water. The scenes were amazing. Boats sailed along the Cornmarket, Victoria Street, St Peter's Street and St James's Street. Police roped off whole streets for fear of looting. Electricity and telephone services failed. And rumour spread that typhoid had broken out in the town.

The flooded print hall at Northcliffe House in Albert Street in May 1932.

May 1932: two views of the flooded Corn Market.

Further afield, the story was the same. By afternoon, the flood stretched in one vast lake from Darley Abbey to Breadsall. Cellars from the Cavendish to the Vulcan Hotel were flooded. At Alvaston, the Derwent flooded Boulton Lane, Harvey Road, Brighton Road and Chambers Street. At Duffield, the little Ecclesbourne became a raging torrent, carrying away animals, furniture and outbuildings. The Duffield telephone operator donned a bathing costume as she made a desperate bid to restore communications in a switchboard that was four feet under water.

Heavy rain had fallen over the Derby area during the previous few days, and on Saturday, 21 May, Derbeians went to bed with the sound of a torrential downpour hammering against their windows. Even so, they could not have imagined the scenes that would greet them by dawn. From the hills around Kedleston, and from the high

A SINGLE ARTICLE AT WHOLESALE PRICE
COX & MALIN LTD
H.SAMUEL
H.SAM
BRANCHES
THE EMPIRE'S LARGEST JEWELLE
YE OLDE ANGEL

ground in Mickleover, along the Littleover and Bramble Brooks, came an avalanche of water. Markeaton Brook surged along its narrow banks until it approached the Gas Works in Ford Street, where the volume was so great that the culvert, constructed 90 years earlier, was incapable of saving Derby this time.

Unable to pass under the bridge, the water swept into the streets, forcing up manhole covers, tearing back tarmac. Part of a wall at St Werburgh's Church was demolished, cassocks, surplices and hymn books ruined. People in Willow Row and Tenant Street were marooned in their bedrooms. The force of the water smashed shop windows in Victoria Street and the Cornmarket. Tailors' dummies floated down the street. At the Midland Drapery, where preparations were under way for the store's 50th anniversary sale, more than £40,000 worth of damage was done to drapery goods and carpets. In the Derwent, two huge logs crashed again and again against the Long Bridge. Two dogs and a pig were seen floating under the Cattle Market Bridge. Even on Osmaston Road, tramcars were unable to run the full length because of the overflow of the brook that ran to Normanton.

Bright afternoon sunshine brought out the sightseers, but the waters still rose. Between 4pm and 7pm, the Derwent rose another 18 inches. And when torrential rain returned during the evening, Corporation workmen struggled heroically to place sandbags in vulnerable areas that had thus far escaped. At Chester Green there was the amazing sight of hundreds of wild rabbits trying to escape by scaling trees.

At last the rains stopped and the waters began to recede. At their highest they had covered plaques which had marked the high-point of the last great flood, in 1842.

Happily, the 1932 flood did not kill – 90 years earlier, Ann Astle had died while trying to escape from her house in Brook Street – but it left behind a huge amount of damage. And a terrible stench that seemed to pervade every corner of Derby for weeks to come.

An estimate of £400,000 worth of damage was not contested. And on Monday, 23 May, a gas explosion at the Cornmarket premises of Samuel's, the jewellers, injured several people. At the

The Morledge, looking towards Tenant Street, flooded in May 1932.

time, the streets were packed with over 50,000 people hoping to buy flood-damaged goods. The *Derby Daily Telegraph's* offices in Albert Street were flooded and the first editions reporting the floods were printed at the sister paper in Leicester.

Derby Town Council opened a flood relief fund. And at last put into operation a scheme to divert Markeaton Brook, so that never again would the townspeople of Derby suffer from the watercourse that had blighted them for centuries.

Derby's two evening newspapers merge

FRIDAY, 29 January 1932 was an historic day in the life of Derby: the costly newspaper war that had seen readers benefit from all sorts of giveaways – even free insurance – had finally drawn to a close. From the following day, the newspapers would merge. Henceforth, the *Derby Daily Telegraph* would rule.

For almost half a century, the *Derby Daily Express* and the *Telegraph* had vied for the town's readership. For much of that time, both had been locally owned. Around three years earlier, however, each had been acquired by rival newspaper groups, the *Telegraph* being owned by the *Daily Mirror* for a few months before being sold on to Northcliffe Newspapers. The *Express* now owned by Allied Northern Newspapers.

In the 1920s, the *Telegraph's* sales had declined, but by 1932 they boasted the bigger circulation in Derby. The *Express* countered by announcing that it was the best-selling newspaper in Derbyshire.

In the interim, it was the readers who had benefited as both papers ran imaginative promotional schemes to attract and keep readers. Free insurance was probably the most popular. Readers registered with a particular newspaper and were then covered, up to £5,000, for a range of accidents: £5 for breaking a leg at home; £1,500 for dying on a passenger ship.

Now there was to be only one evening newspaper in Derby. Allied Northern would close the *Express*, and another paper in

Newspaper rivalry between the Derby Daily Telegraph *and the* Derby Daily Express *saw this display outside the* Telegraph*'s headquarters in Albert Street in 1932.*

Bristol. Northcliffe would shut their evening newspaper in Newcastle-upon-Tyne. The joint newspaper would be published from Northcliffe House in Albert Street, the former Corn Exchange and Palais de Dance into which the *Telegraph* had moved in September 1929, "one of the finest regional newspaper offices in the kingdom".

On Saturday, 30 January 1932, the first issue of the merged papers appeared. The front-page lead story concerned the heroic effort of an LMS worker to save the life of a young neighbour in Rivett Street.

Francis Fryatt, who worked as a smith's striker at the Carriage and Wagon Works, heard screams coming from next door and rushed in to find eight-year-old Elsie Goodman "a ball of fire". Together with her father, Fryatt extinguished the flames with his hands. Then his son, also Francis, picked the girl up and ran with her in his arms for a mile to the DRI, where she died.

It was a tragic way to begin a new era in Derby's newspaper story.

Radio broadcast from Derby

FIVE of the items included the BBC Midland Regional wireless service's "A Derbyshire Week" in November 1932, would actually be broadcast from the town, it was announced. The rest would be broadcast from a Birmingham studio.

So what treats were there in store for listeners?

The massed bands of the Sherwood Foresters Beating The Retreat at the Drill Hall in Becket Street would no doubt have proved popular. So, too, the two Derbyshire dialects plays presented by the village players of Great Hucklow, although as there was no telephone line to the new Florence Nightingale Hall in Holloway, from where it had been hoped to transmit the plays, they had been moved to the Friary Hotel, Derby.

And regional listeners would perhaps have found a talk on "Modern Railways" by Mr D. W. Sandford, relayed from the LMS Works illuminating. Perhaps less so, the offering of Mr A. J.

Aiton, CBE, whose talk to be broadcast from the company's Derby premises was entitled "Flanged Pipes".

Trolley buses instead of trams

IN September 1932, plans were being pushed ahead by Derby Tramways Committee to replace the town's tramcars with trolley buses. It was hoped to complete the trolley service on the Burton Road and Uttoxeter Road routes by the following July, at a cost of £34,000: £24,000 for vehicles and £10,000 for overhead cables and turning points. The Kedleston Road and LMS Station routes would go over from trams to petrol buses when the vehicles were released from Burton Road and Uttoxeter Road. The Normanton route would be converted to trolley buses by the spring of 1934. Extra money was also being made available to alter the Tramways' Osmaston Road depot. The whole scheme would cost ratepayers some £111,000.

"Derby First" exhibition

"DERBY First" was the motto of Derbeians anxious to promote the town's industry and commerce in October 1932. And there was a special guest to help them in their endeavours when film star Molly Lamont made a personal appearance at what was the biggest exhibition of any kind ever held in the town.

The Derby First exhibition at the Drill Hall was opened by the Mayor, Alderman William Salisbury, on a rainy evening that month, but it was the arrival of Miss Lamont, South African-born star of such films as *Strictly Business*, *Brother Alfred* and *Lucky Girl*, which created the biggest stir.

At 7.30pm, she emerged on to the Drill Hall stage into a blaze of spotlights, where, later that evening, mannequins would display "charming, inexpensive models in ladies' wear". In contrast, the film star herself was, according to the *Derby Daily Telegraph*, "tall, golden-haired, wearing an ivory velvet evening dress, a frilled cape coatee with white fox collar, and a long trail of pink carnations."

Having toured the 56 stands, she told the crowds: "I cannot tell you what a pleasure it has given me to come to see the Derby Exhibition. I congratulate the organisers on one of the finest exhibitions I have seen outside London. It makes me feel frightfully homesick, for we have these sorts of exhibitions in South Africa."

The Mayor told her: "In Derby you will find shops comparable with any town of its size in the country." Then to his audience: "I am proud of the quality of goods Derby industry produces and sells. I am proud of the quality of the people who purchase them."

The audience then watched the mannequins parade the latest frocks, coats and underwear from consignments just received by Brindley's and Moults, although Miss Lamont told a *Telegraph* reporter that she had been more interested in electrical and gas equipment for the home, labour-saving devices, and the radio-gramophone stand.

1933

The Royal Show

AS the *Derby Evening Telegraph* of 5 July 1933, commented: "No other town or city in the country can say as much." The writer was referring to the fact that the Royal Show was being held in Derby for the fifth time.

Long before it settled on its permanent site in Stoneleigh, Warwickshire, the Royal Show was taken around the country. And nowhere in the realm could boast of staging it more times than Derby. Alas, what the writer could not know was that this was also the very last time that the town would be so honoured.

The first Royal Show had been held in Oxford in 1839. It first came to Derby in 1843, to Osmaston Park, where all subsequent shows in the town were held. Of course, that Osmaston Park bore no real resemblance to the one we know today, off Osmaston Park Road. This park belonged to the Wilmot Horton family and stood where the Ascot Drive industrial area is now situated.

July 1933: Sadler Gate is decorated for the visit of King George V and Queen Mary.

Derby paint manufacturers, Joseph Mason & Co Ltd, receives a visit from King George V and Queen Mary during the Royal Show held on Osmaston Park in 1933.

The Midland Railway had purchased it in 1888, to house the new Carriage and Wagon works, but a large part was retained for a showground. The Royal Show returned in 1881, 1906 and 1921. Now, in the early years of the 1930s, it was back once more. And how Derby celebrated in the sunshine and temperatures of 85 degrees.

Thousands cheered as King George V and Queen Mary were driven through the streets in an open-topped carriage. As the *Telegraph* put it: "The old borough of Derby lived today a story which might have been lifted straight out of a book of fairy tales when, beneath a canopy of blues skies, amidst a blaze of colour, and with stately pageantry and splendour, the King and Queen paid their official visit to the Royal Show at Osmaston."

The report continued: "Derby gave their Majesties a Royal welcome as they drove through the heart of the town in an open semi-state coach drawn by two magnificent greys, along a route lined ten, 20 and 30 deep with cheering citizens, past cottages and mansions, and offices and shops, and works, every window of which was framed with eager and smiling faces.

"From Allestree to Alvaston, the Royal route was gay with flowers, flags and bunting ... There was a festive spirit even about the early business buses into the town this morning. Many of the 'world's workers' were missing from their places and instead there were girls in gay dresses ...The majority of Derby men wore buttonholes ranging from a pink or a rose to a tricolour rosette."

The King and Queen had arrived in Derby by car from Chatsworth. At Derwent Park they exchanged the internal combustion engine for real horsepower and then swept on into town, down Queen Street and into the Market Place, where police, solders and members of the British Legion held thousands of people back.

The band of the 5th Battalion, Sherwood Foresters, played the National Anthem and then the Royal couple were on their way again, up St Peter's Street, The Spot and down London Road before arriving at the showground at 12.50pm, when they met members of the Royal Show committee and toured the exhibits.

Then they were on their way and, soon afterwards, Derby also said goodbye to the Royal Show for good.

Problems caused by cinemas

IN 1933, Derby's wayward youth would have been less of a problem if cinemas had been allowed to open on Sundays. But better lighting was needed to prevent people from "cuddling and canoodling" at the pictures. That was the view of the chief constable, Colonel Horatio Rawlings, when he addressed a luncheon held in the town by the Derbyshire branch of the National Council of Women. He told them: "I believe I am correct in stating that cinema proprietors in Derby have no desire to open on Sundays. Personally, I think that is a very good thing, although I should not oppose cinemas opening from, say, 8pm to 10pm, so long as the shows were of the right type.

"For this reason. There are many young people who wander about the streets on Sunday, who will not go to a church or chapel, and it would be better, especially on wintry nights, if they had some place to go where they could see plays or films of educational value."

He listed the sort of films he would like to see – "delightful travel films, news, sport, nature, and certain advertisements which showed the manufacture of certain commodities cannot be rated too highly" – but blamed films showing "sumptuous conditions, which could not be kept by king or emperor," for making discontent "which might breed a rebel spirit against the social order".

Rawlings spoke of some films which in the last year had been rejected by the censor: "One wonders that human beings would descend to such a state of moral degradation as to place themselves in such situations for the purpose of having a photograph taken. Most of these films were Continental; some were American."

Censoring films was another difficult matter in the 1930s, according to Colonel Rawlings: "It is ridiculous to expect that an official should be placed at the door of a cinema to ask the age of suspected youthful persons.

"There is an onus on the parents and I think that a good many parents not exercise their power."

As an instance of the way in which local control in Derby sometimes ran counter to the feelings of the police, Colonel Rawlings explained that he had voted against one particular film being shown, but that there was a majority for it.

The voting had occurred after the local body controlling cinemas exercised its right to see a film privately after the censor had given his decision and to judge for itself whether it was fit for public exhibition.

Said Rawlings: "The film had no educational value – and probably did some harm." He did not tell us what it was.

Derby's chief constable was also concerned about courting couples.

"I have a strong objection to seeing people cuddling and canoodling in the cinema. It annoys me to see people making fools of themselves in the audience. It is all right on the stage, but the free entertainment annoys me. Light would obviate that type of thing."

Remarkable sequel to Derby will dispute – and the case of the stolen parsley

THE 1930s produced some often-bizarre court cases in Derby, none more so than in March 1933 when a dispute over a will ended with three of the protagonists being "roped in" to a Mickleover house while the police were called. That month, husband and wife, Herbert and Leah Oliver, and Arthur Perry, who lived at Lord Street, Allenton, were up before Derby County Police Court, charged with breaking and entering the house of a bus cleaner, Joseph Bayliss, at Alma Cottages on the main Derby-Mickleover road.

It was the result of a long-running dispute. The court heard that in 1915, Mr Bayliss, who was in the army at the time, had married. Four years later, he and his wife split up, and in 1920 he moved in with a Mrs Green, who had recently left her husband. Herbert Palmer was Mrs Green's son, and when she died in 1932, Mr Bayliss had produced a will that showed that his common law wife had left everything to him.

Palmer, however, claimed that there was an earlier will and produced a letter from the Derby solicitors, Flint, Marsden and Bishop, containing a copy of this, which shows that her son was also a beneficiary.

Bayliss duly gave Palmer a fur coat once belonging to his mother, and there he thought the matter had ended. But while he was visiting Leeds – after first giving a neighbour the keys to look after his cat and parrot – the Palmers and their friend, Arthur Perry, broke into his house and removed some furniture.

The neighbour who had been entrusted with the key got her husband to rope the door, with the Palmers and Perry still inside, and when PC Sharpe of the local constabulary arrived, he arrested the trio.

Not surprisingly, the five magistrates hearing the case soon tired of the nonsense and dismissed it.

The same month, Derby magistrates also dismissed another case –this time involving some stolen parsley. Horace Smith was accused to stealing the parsley belonging to Arthur Turner of

Chellaston. Smith had been spotted digging up the herb on Mr Turner's allotment.

He admitted all, pleaded that he was a married man and had been out of work for 12 months, and promised "to go straight in the future". The magistrates sent him packing on him renewing his promise not to reoffend. Meanwhile, the parsley growers of Chellaston could sleep soundly in their beds.

1934

The bus conductor who saved an aircraft pilot

THE end of the town's electric trams, the official opening of Markeaton Lake, two new cinemas on London Road, a scorching summer, some significant transfer news for the Rams – and the Trent bus conductor whose quick-thinking helped a lost pilot find his bearings. They were some of the highlights for the people of Derby in 1934.

It was in March that year when the *Derby Evening Telegraph* received a letter from Alan Wallace, writing from the Caledonian Club in London's St James's Square: "When I was flying over the Derby district, the visibility was extremely bad due to low cloud and haze.

"I was greatly assisted by a bus conductor and driver for their thoughtfulness and presence of mind. I was trying to find my exact whereabouts at the 'Y' in the main road, and the driver of a red bus, anticipating my difficulty, stopped.

"Either he or the conductor got out and displayed a large destination board with the word 'Derby' painted in large letters. He pointed it along one of three roads. The board I read easily, and proceeded without further difficulty."

In fact it was the bus conductor, Alfred Martin of Crewe Street, Derby, who pointed the way. He told the *Telegraph*: "I was working on the Alfreton to Derby route with driver Sid Cholerton of Walter

Street in Derby. I noticed that the plane had followed us from Kilburn and I got the idea that he wanted to know where he was.

"The pilot was flying very low, just above the trees, and kept banking as if he was trying to read the destination board on the bus. When we got to Coxbench, Sid stopped the bus and I held the board up and pointed out the way to Derby. I had an idea he wanted to land and thought the Racecourse would be a good place."

Goodbye to our trams

THE same month, public transport was again in the news when the last of Derby's electric trams went out of service. The decision to replace trams with trolley buses dated back to a town council meeting in August 1929. It was a far from unanimous decision, however. Concerns were raised that, because trolley buses could run only where there were overhead wires, they would show the same inflexibility as the trams they were replacing. But the arguments for their introduction were overwhelming. Apart from enjoying, like the trams, an almost free source of power from the municipal power station – money would simply be transferred from Corporation department to another – maintenance would be cheaper, and there would be no vibration, hardly any noise, and a reduced fire risk.

So trolley buses were introduced until, by 17 March 1934, only the town centre to Pear Tree and Normanton routes were still served by trams. That night, Derby's last regular electric tram service rattled down Normanton Road, although it wasn't quite the end of the trams themselves.

Works services along Osmaston Road survived until 30 June, and the official departure date for Derby' trams was set for 2 July, when Car 78 was taken to Victoria Street and photographed alongside one of the new trolleys. Then the tram destination board was set to "Osmaston Road Car Depot" and track-based public transport in Derby rattled off up to The Spot and into history.

A few tramcars survived as sheds on Derby allotments, and even a changing room at Homelands School. The majority, though, went to the breaker's yard.

The junction of the Corn Market, St Peter's Street and Victoria Street is a tangle of trolleybus wires.

By the end of 1934, however, Derby's public transport was coming in for some thunderous criticism in the pages of the *Evening Telegraph*.

Signing themselves "All the Way", one reader wrote: "May I lodge a complaint in your valuable columns about the inability of the Derby omnibus department to cater properly for shoppers on Friday afternoons." Apparently, when the 4.30pm to Littleover Lane eventually arrived at the Spot, there were so many people waiting that around 50 – including the letter writer – were left at the stop.

"Felix" complained about the unreliability of the Slack Lane service, asking: Why was the 12.40pm from the Wardwick always late? Why was there not a barrier to enable 'first-come-first-served? And why were all the worn-out buses used on the route? Unsurprisingly, no one at the council was available to comment.

Leisurely times

IN the same letters column, "Another Theatre Lover" complained that the Grand Theatre in Babington Lane was failing to employ first-class actors, forcing the writer to go to Nottingham and Birmingham to watch well-performed plays. And "Annoyed Visitor" had parked their car outside the King's Hall, on their way to a dance, and been bothered by young boys asking to "look after" it. After telling them to clear off, the driver had returned to find these "imps" had apparently jammed the self-starter.

For those Derbeians preferring their entertainment to be a little less demanding than tripping the light fantastic around a dance floor, two new cinemas opened in the town in 1934.

Derby's Gaumont Palace was the county's first true purpose-built "super cinema". Standing on London Road – the building is now the Cosmo restaurant – the Gaumont was built from scratch, unlike the Coliseum, further down London Road, which, although advertising itself as "Derby's New Super Cinema", was in fact a converted Congregational church.

The souvenir programme which marked the Gaumont's opening reminded patrons: "Twelve months ago, a number of rather dingy old buildings stood on this ground. Since then, the builders, with their army of 200 men, have wrought mightily and skilfully with the 500 tons of steel, the million bricks, the 5,000 tons of concrete, and the thousand and one other materials which are the bones, body and clothing of the Gaumont Palace."

For those of a sporting nature, both Derby County and Derbyshire CCC were enjoying successful times. Interest in the Rams was such that, when Wolverhampton Wanderers visited the Baseball Ground for an FA Cup tie in January 1934, a record crowd of 37,727 packed in.

Two players coming to Derby were Reg Stockill, the Arsenal inside-forward manager George Jobey signed in September for £2,000; and Scottish international centre-forward, Hughie Gallacher, who cost nearly £3,000 from Chelsea in November. A player on his way out was Rams skipper, and England full-back, Tommy Cooper, who was transferred to Liverpool for £8,000 in December.

Derbyshire's cricketers, meanwhile, enjoyed the blazing summer – in July, temperatures in Derby touched almost 90 degrees – by winning a club record 12 matches to finish third in the table. In October, local motor racing fans who went to Donington Park to see the first international 100-mile road race ever to be run in England were treated to some thrilling racing on a track made doubly treacherous by water and – long before the railway companies had thought of it – fallen leaves.

In July, Markeaton Park Lake was officially opened. The park itself had been open to the people of Derby since 1931; now Markeaton Brook had been widened to provide a boating lake, half a mile long and between 20 to 80 yards wide.

This and that

EARLIER in 1934, local trades unionists had marked the centenary of the Derby Turnout – the historic strike of silk workers that had a direct bearing on the advancement of the trades union movement. And Derby lost a stalwart of the Labour movement when Alderman W. H. Sailsbury, a former mayor, died in January, aged only 52.

The death also occurred of William Wright Bemrose, for 50 years connected with the Derby printers, Bemrose & Sons, and former CO of the Territorial 5th Battalion, Sherwood Foresters.

In 1934, you could buy a new semi-detached house on Chain Lane, Littleover, for £450, a detached villa overlooking Chaddesden Park for £600, or you could "live in an orchard at Alvaston" where semi-detached houses cost £395 freehold, payable in easy weekly instalments of 10s 8d.

If driving was your fancy, the Unity Garage on Burton Road was offering the new Talbot 65 Saloon motorcar – with self-changing accelerating gearbox – for £395. Or perhaps you would have fancied a new Vauxhall Six from Oscroft's of King Street: £195 for a 12hp model.

Whatever, judging by the *Telegraph's* letters page, it seems unlikely that, 80 years ago, you would have put your faith in Derby's public transport system.

1935

Royal celebrations – and some town planning

EIGHTY years ago, working folk across Britain were not accustomed to being handed extra time off without pay. Indeed, there had long been a battle raging to make any kind of paid holiday an entitlement. But on 6 May 1935, to mark the fact that King George V and Queen Mary had been on the throne for 25 years, workers everywhere enjoyed a day off with pay, on what was officially designated Silver Jubilee Day

Derbyshire was determined to join in and make the most of perfect weather, and towns and villages across the county organised galas, sports events and displays, while Boy Scouts lit a series of beacons that made a fiery chain from north to south. Many communities were decorated with coloured lights.

John Clark, the Mayor of Derby, held a silver jubilee reception for Derbyshire's leading citizens. And as the Guildhall was not big enough, and the Council House project hardly on the drawing

Derby Market Place pictured in the late 1930s when a small car park was provided in front of the Guildhall.

board, the mayor had to use Bemrose School, then five years old, to stage his event.

On a more mundane, but nevertheless vital, note, in 1935 Derby Town Council announced that it would spend £568,000 on an improved drainage system for the borough. The cornerstones were laid for the new £50,000 police courts and offices on the corner of Derwent Street – part of the Central Improvement Scheme that was transforming that part of Derby – and the *Evening Telegraph* made much of the fact that a wireless room would be installed at the police station to communicate with patrol cars.

Traffic was concerning Derbeians in 1935. A census showed that in one week, no less than 143,397 vehicles passed down St Peter's Street, compared with 101,841 four years earlier. The *Telegraph* reported that there were "striking plans" to relieve the town's traffic problem.

"With the completion in 1933 of the section from Uttoxeter New Road to Duffield Road, a span of six miles of circular route linked up London and the South with Matlock and the North.

"Town planning arrangements now provide that the link from London Road to Nottingham Road will eventually continue through Chaddesden to Mansfield Road, near the Isolation Hospital, and then across the river via Darley Grove to Duffield Road... the full circular route embracing the whole town will be complete."

The thought that a new Derby airport would be built at Radbourne still persisted: "Another big development was the provision of a site for an aerodrome at Radbourne. In view of the town's geographical position... a municipal aerodrome would be a vital necessity to Derby in the future. The initial cost of the scheme is £113,000, and the site of 200 acres, said to be an admirable one, had past all in the Air Ministry tests."

Derby's various local government undertakings were certainly booming in 1935. The council-owned electricity department, with its 40,000 consumers, reported a profit of almost £36,000. The new trolley bus system had made nearly £11,000 on the year. The water department's profit was over £8,000, and the markets department's over £4,000.

Party politics

THREE local politicians were made Freemen of Derby to celebrate the local government centenary: Alderman W. G. Wilkins, the "father" of the council which he had first joined in 1894, had twice served as Derby's mayor; Alderman Oswald Ling was also a former mayor, and leader of the Conservative Party; and Alderman W.R. Raynes, who would give his name to part of the Ring Road, was a former Derby MP and the town's first Labour mayor.

Despite Conservative gains in local elections, Derby Town Council was still controlled by Labour. And in the General Election, National Party candidates J. H. "Jimmy" Thomas (completing 25 years as a Derby MP) and W. Allan Reid, were returned to Parliament by Derby's voters.

On the weather front, Derby enjoyed a scorching summer in 1935, with the hottest day coming on 13 July when the temperature reached almost 90 degrees. The hot weather ran through May to August, by which time Derby was five inches behind its annual rainfall. In September, however, nearly one and a third inches of rain fell on one day alone. The month's final quota – 4.19 inches – was double the average for that month, and October's record was four inches. In December came the snow and ice.

Industrial prowess

IN the 21st century we take video conferencing for granted, although it seems only a few years ago that even telephone conferencing was an unusual way to conduct business meetings. In 1935, however, the Derby firm of International Combustion landed a £300,000 contract with the Government of Western Australia, thanks to what was referred to in the *Evening Telegraph* as "radio-telephone conferences" between the firm and its overseas representatives.

Later in the year, a second radio-telephone conference linked up International Combustion with buyers in Australia, Africa, India, New Zealand, South America, Paris and New York. It seemed to work. The *Evening Telegraph* reported: "Orders obtained for Derby from the Dominions showed a marked increase following the new departure in trading methods."

A notable trading change took place in 1935 when the Royal Crown Derby Porcelain Company on Osmaston Road absorbed the Old Crown Derby China Works in King Street.

Long-serving workers at Ley's Foundry were rewarded when 43 past and present employees with 40 or more years' service to the company were each given £5 and a framed certificate. Sir Gordon Ley unveiled a bronze tablet – paid for by workers and placed outside the mess room in Colombo Street – to the memory of Ian F. Panton, the Ley's works general manager who had died at the age of 46.

Other local deaths in 1935 included that of Oliver Platteau, head of Derby's Belgian colony, who had lived in the town since he was exiled from Antwerp during the First World War and who had acted as the district's unofficial Belgian consul.

Taking advantage of our beautiful countryside

IN 1935 Derby's children lost a good friend with the death of Mr H. J. Blount, who, as secretary of the Pearson Fresh Air Fund, had organised for over 60,000 local boys and girls to pay visits to the seaside and to the country. They might have visited some of the most beautiful parts of Derbyshire steadily be added to the areas preserved by the National Trust and the Council for the Preservation of Rural England.

Secured for the pleasure of the public were the Longshaw estate (765 acres), Alport Height (nine acres), Blackamoor (448 acres), Taddington Woods (50 acres), parts of Dovedale (330 acres), Shining Cliff Woods at Alderwasley (200 acres) and Stanton Moor Edge (28 acres). Ilam Hall, Dovedale, became the latest addition to the chain of Derbyshire Youth Hostels, after being presented to the National Trust by Mr R. McDougall, a well-known Lancashire businessman.

During 1935 there were 30,000 visits to Peakland hostels, 10,000 more than in the previous year.

One area that looked like being out of bounds, however, was the village of Derwent that, it was announced, would be submerged when the Derwent Valley Water Board's Ladybower reservoir was completed. That was still five years ago, but the £750,000 contract had been awarded in the autumn of 1935, to a Scottish company. The reservoir would ultimately submerge Derwent village, a church, surrounding farms and a main road. But then Derby alone was consuming 5.6m gallons of water every day. It had to come from somewhere.

Culture, proud soldiery – and a new bishop

Derby was also awash with cultural events in 1935. In November, the great tenor, John McCormack, gave a concert at the Grand Theatre in Babington Lane, in aid of the Derbyshire Royal Infirmary. On the brink of world fame, Arthur Rubenstein, the Polish-born pianist, gave a recital as one of the season's chamber concerts at Derby. And the legendary comedian, Sir Harry Lauder, took time off from appearing at the Grand Theatre to address members of Derby Rotary Club.

Ashbourne achieved wider fame when a BBC wireless programme was broadcast from the town. Items included talks by a clockmaker, a farmer, two schoolboys, a caretaker, two Shrovetide football celebrities and an angling authority. The story of the so-called grammar school, ghost was also included in the programme.

Derby also played its part in making local radio history in 1935. When the Association of the British Chambers of Commerce held their first meeting in the town since 1883, a banquet was laid at the LMS Railway Institute, from where speeches were relayed by the BBC to the Dominions and Colonies, It was the first time that speeches in Derby had been broadcast to the Empire.

For the county's soldiery came the welcome news that the 1st Battalion, Sherwood Foresters, were being posted to "the best station in the British Empire". The 1st Foresters were to replace the 1st Manchesters in the West Indies. The 2nd Battalion, meanwhile, was returning to Lichfield after foreign duty since 1919.

Finally, Derby had a new bishop. The first incumbent, the Right Reverend Edmund Courtenay Pearce, died in October after collapsing while taking a confirmation service near Glossop. His successor was the Venerable Alfred Edward John Rawlinson, the brilliant 51-year-old academic who had been Bishop of Auckland. He would hold the post until 1959.

1936

The King is dead ...

THE first new of King George V's fatal illness reached Derby on Friday, 17 January, when the *Derby Evening Telegraph* revealed that there was a rapid renewal of his bronchial catarrh, followed by

Derby folk queue to see the wreath being sent on behalf of the town to the funeral of King George V in January 1936.

The Duchess of Gloucester visits the Derbyshire Royal Infirmary in 1936 to lay the foundation stone to a new extension of the hospital.

concern over the king's heart condition. At 9.25pm on Monday, 20 January came the now-famous bulletin: "The King's life is moving peacefully towards its close." George V died at five minutes to midnight on the same day. The news was released at 12.16am, and the *Evening Telegraph* rushed out an early-morning edition, its front page edged in black. A second special edition later that day devoted most of its pages to the king's life and his visits to Derbyshire, not least to attend the Royal Show on Osmaston Park three years earlier.

The *Telegraph's* attention then turned to the new monarch, Edward VIII, and his Derbyshire connections. The newspaper reminded readers that, when he was the Prince of Wales, he had visited Derbyshire several times. In 1928, Derby had provided the prince with a particularly memorable welcome after he had first gone to Ashbourne to throw up the ball for the world-famous annual Shrovetide football match.

By the end of the year, Edward was no longer king. For months his affair with the American divorcee, Wallis Simpson, had been public knowledge in the USA and Europe, but the British press had had their silence until a former vicar of St Werburgh's Church in Derby – Dr Alfred Blunt, now the Bishop of Bradford – made an oblique reference to it at his diocesan conference. Edward's shy brother, Bertie was now King George VI. He, too, had visited Derbyshire on many occasions.

The county enjoyed several royal visits in 1936. As guests of Sir William and Noreen Bass, the Princess Royal attended Derby Races in November. The same month, the Duke and Duchess of Gloucester were guests of Sir Ian Walker at Osmaston Manor, for a pheasant shoot.

The duchess had been in Derby the previous month when she laid the foundation stone of the £100,000 extension to the Derbyshire Royal Infirmary. And toys donated by the Duke of Kent for distribution to children of Derbyshire's unemployed were allocated to 20 welfare centres around the county.

The Jimmy Thomas scandal

ON the political front there was a national sensation that reverberated locally. In 1929, Jimmy Thomas, the former railwayman and trades unionist, had been made an Honorary Freeman of Derby, and in 1935 – in recognition of his 25 years' service as a Labour MP of the town – he was presented with a gold watch and chain, a Royal Crown Derby dinner service for his wife, and £2,750 which he donated to Derby's hospitals.

Now, however, his career was to end in the most remarkable scandal. While serving as Colonial Secretary he was accused of passing Budget secrets to a friend and to another MP. A judicial tribunal found him guilty and he had little option but to resign his Derby seat. In the Parliamentary by-election that followed – the first in the town's history – Philip Noel-Baker was elected for Labour.

For one politician, however 1936 was a happy year. In November, Conservative councillor Mrs Elizabeth Petty was elected Derby's first female mayor. Mrs Petty, an early member of National Council for Women, had joined the Town Council in 1922. After she became mayor, no one was quite sure how to address her. In the end she happily settled for "Mr Mayor", like all her predecessors. Elected an alderman in 1937, she continued as such until her death, ten years later.

Derby – the boomtown

DERBY was sharing in a national upturn in trading fortunes in 1936; in fact, it was doing rather better than most. Those members of Derby and Derbyshire Chamber of Trade and Commerce engaged in engineering reported increased business without exception. Roll-Royce reported a profit of almost £350,000 compared to £291,000 in 1935.

In June 1936, unemployment in Derby dropped to 2,178, its lowest since 1929. By the end of the year, Derby could boast one of the smallest percentages of unemployment in Britain. Even Derby County made a profit: £14,123 7s 3d, double that of the previous year. Derby Corporation was also in the money, announcing several big spending projects including a £200,000 extension to the Technical College, a new secondary school for girls on Normanton Road, an extension to the nurses' home at the City Hospital, and several road improvement schemes.

Plans were also passed to build 1,000 houses on the Roe Farm Estate, and in February the council also opened its brand-new police courts and office building in Derwent Street. This was the third stage of the Central Improvement Scheme that itself would eventually cost more than £600,000 according to the *Derby Evening Telegraph*.

Details of a traffic census carried out on three sites in Derby revealed that St Mary's Bridge had the greatest amount of traffic overall, but that Siddals Road carried the most pedal cyclists, closely followed by Macklin Street.

More exciting, so far as Derby's transport buffs were concerned, was the August visit of Mr Thomas Campbell Black's "Empire Air Display" at the Stenson Road Flying Ground.

Derbyshire's last VC

NEWS of the late Godfrey Meynell's Victoria Cross had come on Christmas Eve 1935. Captain Meynell, of Meynell Langley, had been awarded the VC for his courage in an action against Pathan tribesmen on India's North-West Frontier while he was serving in the Indian Army. He is still the Derby area's most recent recipient of the nation's highest award for valour – and he won it while there was no actual war taking place. His widow, Sophia, received her husband's medal from King Edward VIII, one of the few investitures carried out by the short-reigning monarch.

For men of the 2nd Battalion, Sherwood Foresters, 1936 was a memorable year, too. The battalion arrived home after 17 years of overseas duty including postings in India and Egypt.

Fire and frost

ONE of the most disastrous fires of the year came on 26 May when the 17th-century Green Man public house at the rear of St Peter's Church in St Peter's Street was destroyed. At the time it was a lovely brick building with a Dutch gable and was run by Offilers, the Derby brewery. It was eventually rebuilt but, alas, had lost most of its charm.

In 1936 the Derby area was badly affected by adverse weather conditions.

Following a gale that caused considerable damage in January, there was a severe frost, much to the delight of the town's skaters who enjoyed 10 days' uninterrupted sport. Others were not so lucky. Since 1927, fog, frost and snow had caused the loss of no less

The 17th-century Green Man public house, at the rear of St Peter's Church in St Peter's Street, was destroyed by fire in May 1936.

than 21 days' horseracing at Derby and in 1936 there were further abandonments at the racecourse on Nottingham Road.

In November, one of the worst fogs for years caused severe disruption to bus and train services. Visibility in Derby's streets was down to a few feet, the fog mingling with smoke from thousands of coal fires.

The hottest day of the years was 21 June, when the temperature reached 81.5F.

Derbyshire champions

Amateur skipper Arthur Richardson led Derbyshire to the first and so far only County Cricket Championship title in their history

ONE major sporting triumph could be celebrated in 1936: the winning, for the first time in the club's history, of the County Cricket Championship by Derbyshire. The team had been threatening for several years, their wonderfully balanced side – almost all of who were born within the county boundary – more than a match for most opponents. Led by amateur captain Arthur Richardson, of the Derby tanning family, and with players of the calibre of Stan Worthington, Harry Storer, Dennis Smith, Bill Copson, Tommy Mitchell, Harry Elliott and Leslie Townsend, Derbyshire swept all before them.

In 1936, Derbyshire upheld its claim to longevity when Mrs Hannah Stretton celebrated her 102nd birthday. A native of the county, she could remember Florence Nightingale living near Matlock, and she had been a passenger on the first train ever to run between Derby and Belper.

1937

Alarming start to the Coronation

THOSE Derbeians walking along Siddals Road on the morning of Wednesday, 12 May 1937, and who hadn't properly read the previous day's *Derby Evening Telegraph*, would probably have been alarmed by a series of loud explosions nearby. The *Telegraph* news item they might have missed would have explained all: on Siddals Field, the military were sounding a 31-gun royal salute.

For even if the finer detail might have passed some by, there was surely nobody in Derby who wasn't aware that this was Coronation Day, the moment that the shy, stammering young Duke of York, known to his family as Bertie, would be crowned a reluctant monarch after the abdication of brother, Edward VIII.

In Derbyshire, preparations to mark the coronation of King George VI, as Bertie would be known, had begun early in the year. Now, there wasn't a town, village or hamlet in the county that

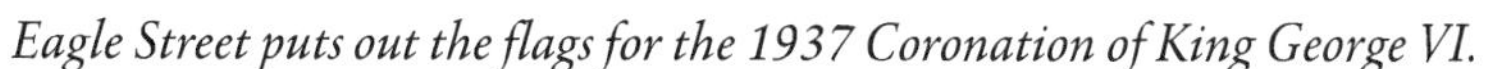

Eagle Street puts out the flags for the 1937 Coronation of King George VI.

Another of the hundreds of Derby streets that were festooned with flags and bunting to celebrate the 1937 Coronation.

wasn't celebrating in style as, all across the area, employees enjoyed a day's holiday, most of them with pay.

In Derby itself, celebrations were held in each of the town's five parks, every child was presented with a souvenir mug or beaker, blind people were given monetary gifts, and there were street parties, celebrations in church halls, and entertainment of every description.

The streets were bedecked with miles of garlands and bunting, while the religious observances included an impressive civic service at Derby Cathedral. The actual service at Westminster was broadcast live and, for the first time in history, the people of Derbyshire heard a British monarch speak on the very day of their coronation. Many Coronation Medals were awarded to local public representatives and members of the police force, permanent memorials were erected in many parts of Derbyshire, and hundreds of Coronation trees planted.

In May, various parties of local people had visited the capital, 400 of them on a special railway excursion organised by the *Telegraph*.

Back to the day itself, a spectacular military parade involving hundreds of soldiers and ex-servicemen was held on the Derwent Street car park. Every local regiment, Territorial unit, and old comrades' association was represented. And, of course, there was that 31-gun salute.

More Royal visits

DURING the course of 1937, Derbyshire welcomed three members of the Royal Family. In April, at Bolsover, the Duke of Kent opened the world's largest plant for making smokeless fuel. In November, the Princess Royal paid yet another visit to Derby Races, accompanied by the Earl of Harewood. The royal party, guests of Sir William Bass, were driven to the Racecourse from the LMS Station. And in February, Princess Helena Victoria, another of Queen Victoria's grandchildren, came to Derby to unveil the Princess Elizabeth cot, paid for by subscribers, at the children's ward at the Derbyshire Royal Infirmary.

Another royal connection came at Alvaston, where the branch headquarters of the local British Legion were opened in premises formerly belonging to the London Road Congregational Church. The king who was never crowned, now the Duke of Windsor, gave permission for the building to be renamed Windsor House.

Continued prosperity – and some politics

CORONATION Year had also seen another period of greater prosperity for local businesses. The Derby and Derbyshire Chamber of Commerce again reported good results for engineering companies, but now local textile manufacturers, especially those engaged in the production of artificial silk, shared in the boom. Orders connected with the Coronation itself saw annual turnovers grow rapidly.

In engineering, International Combustion made a profit of £170,150, an increase of more than £55,000 on 1936. The company now had enough work on its books to provide full employment for the next two years.

This was all good news for workers. British Celanese gave its employees a decent pay rise, as did Rolls-Royce, although a three-week strike by grinders at Royces had resulted in temporary stoppages that affected thousands of other workers there. And a meeting in Derby in November, between Derbyshire mine owners and the Derbyshire Miners' Association, agreed on a new wage structure and provision for a holiday saving fund. In July, there were only 1,903 wholly unemployed in Derby, compared to 10,500 in December 1931.

Derby Corporation was also busy in 1937, approving plans for the new £200,000 Council House, on land bounded by Derwent Street, Corporation Street and the new Open Market, and reporting that work was well under way on the £600,000 plan to improve Derby's main drainage scheme.

At Burnaston, meanwhile, in one of her last engagements as Derby's first woman mayor, Mrs Elizabeth Petty cut the first sod on the site of the town's new municipal airport. Over 138,000 acres, the minimum Air Ministry requirement were being developed at a cost of more than £20,000. Developments like a fog-landing runway were going to be left for future consideration, but it was hoped that Burnaston House would be converted into a clubhouse or a centre for airmen undergoing training courses.

Other 1937 plans for Derby will strike a familiar chord today. Work on Town Planning Road No 4 – London Road to Nottingham Road – was progressing satisfactorily as Derby pushed on with its ring road. The road would be a duel carriageway, 100ft wide, and open up an area covered by something called the Riverlands scheme.

The Town Council remained under Labour's control, but only after polling in 16 wards left them with a majority of just two seats.

Labour's 33 representatives faced 26 Conservatives, four Liberals and one member of the Independent Labour Party. The new mayor in succession to Mrs Petty was Alderman Edward Ernest Paulson, who had entered the council in 1921. Labour's bid to gain control of the county council failed when they lost three seats and their 23 councillors lined up against 47 anti-Socialists.

In September 1937, A. F. Sidgreaves, managing director of Rolls-Royce, opened a £25,500 extension to Derby Technical College on Normanton Road. With the opening of the new premises, the old ones, on Green Lane, were given over to the School of Art. There were also extensions to the DRI – where 40,000 "Coronation bricks", each bearing the new king's name, where incorporated into the walls – and a new nurses' home adjoining the Derbyshire Women's Hospital in the Friar Gate area.

Mining disasters and other fatalities

UNDERLINING Derbyshire's mining traditions – and the dangers therein – there were several pit disasters this year. In January, at Duckmanton near Chesterfield, nine men were killed in an explosion at Markham Colliery, a mine owned by the Staveley Coal and Iron Company. Seven men lost their lives following an explosion at South Normanton Colliery in February. And nine men were injured, three of them seriously, when there was an explosion at the coke ovens at Grassmoor Colliery in May.

One worker was also killed, and seven injured, in February when steel blown from a converter at the Parker Foundry on Mansfield Road fell on the men. In sport, there was a fatality when two cars crashed into a wall during a 12-hour sports car race at Donington Park in July.

Sport and leisure

DERBY County finished fourth in the old First Division in 1936-37, eight points behind the champions, Manchester City, who scored 107 goals and conceded 61 in the process. Chesterfield were enjoying some rare heady days, playing Second Division football – they finished 15th but were ahead of Nottingham Forest. Burton Town reached the second round of the FA Cup, beating fellow non-Leaguers, Wigan Athletic, in the process.

For local cinemagoers there was another venue to take in when the £30,000 Cavendish cinema opened on the site of the old Pavilion music hall that had burned down in 1929. The Pavilion had been erected in 1908 by Offiler's brewery, who also owned the Cavendish Hotel pub opposite, which they had opened not long before. Now an Offiler's director, Cecil Offiler, had a seat on the board of the new Cavendish Picture House (Derby) Ltd.

As the year ended, many Derbeians looked forward to some LMS railway excursions on New Year's Day, 1938. There were long day trips to Carlisle, Edinburgh, Dumfries, Glasgow and Greenock, and to York, Darlington, Thornaby, Middlesbrough, West Hartlepool and Whitley Bay. A half-day excursion had also been arranged to London, and an evening trip to Manchester.

Alas, when the fun had ended, along with the rest of Britain, Derbeians were to face months of almost unbearable tension.

A 'Sam' cartoon published in the Derby Evening Telegraph, *July 1937.*

1938

Gathering storm

THE year 1938 saw Derby undergoing great changes. The Central Improvement Plan was well under way and each month seemed to see further development and redevelopment throughout the town and out into the county, from new refuse and communication provisions, to a new home for the Borough Council.

But the optimism generated by such improvements was punctuated by tragedy and mourning – the deaths of 79 miners at Markham and the loss of the greatly-loved 9th Duke of Devonshire – and entirely overshadowed by the frightening spectre of another world war.

As the political situation in Europe worsened, and the threat of war seemed ever closer, national and local authorities were stepping up their efforts to prepare the country for the expected conflict ahead. The Air Ministry was already preparing for the worst and Derby Borough Council had agreed to sell the Ministry some 55 acres of land on the "Riverlands", for the establishment of a £100,000 barrage balloon depot to defend against aerial attack. This would provide buildings for the inflated balloons, a training ground, workshops and dwellings for the men working at the depot.

In April, Derby marked "Protection Week" – a drive to make townspeople aware of the new air-raid precautions that were to be implemented in case of war. Some 26,000 leaflets were distributed and films encouraging new recruits to the civil defence authority were shown. Over 100,000 homes received a booklet entitled "The Protection of Your Home Against Air-raids". As part of the national preparations, on 7 August an area of the Midlands stretching more than 100 miles, and including Derby, was subject to an experimental 'blackout' for two hours between 1 a.m. and 3 a.m. This was to allow home defence exercises by the RAF.

When Prime Minister Neville Chamberlain returned from Munich clutching his piece of paper – the agreement he had

British Prime Minister Neville Chamberlain and Derby County manager George Jobey were discussing defence problem in the Derby Evening Telegraph, *March 1939 as seen by 'Sam'.*

made with Hitler – many genuinely believed that war had been averted. In accordance with this new optimism, loudspeaker vans toured Derby stating that the distribution of gas masks would be immediately halted. In the county, masks already delivered to towns and villages would be handed out, but the consignments for other parishes were to be held in storage for the time being. War preparedness, however, was not entirely abandoned and throughout Derbyshire, the digging of trenches for air-raid protection continued unabated.

In October, it was announced that, should evacuation from the larger cities prove necessary, 90,386 evacuees could be accommodated throughout Derbyshire, each with their own room. If two out of every five evacuees shared a room, this could be expanded to 204,145 displaced people. In combination, it was judged, the counties of Derbyshire, Lancashire and Cheshire could provide emergency accommodation for 611,400 people from Liverpool, Bootle and Manchester.

Troublesome weather, film stars, and a famous aviatrix

WHILE the war now seemed less of a threat, troublesome weather conditions brought chaos to Derbyshire. After a dry beginning to the year – one of the driest on record – with barely five inches of rain in the first four months, heavy rains struck in early summer. On 1 July, a severe thunderstorm hit Derby and one and a half inches of rain, accompanied by snow and hail, fell to earth in less than two hours. In August 12 cows were killed by lightning while sheltering from a thunderstorm under an elm tree at Isley Walton.

Amy Johnson, the famous aviatrix, enjoyed better conditions for her visit to the headquarters of the Derbyshire and Lancashire Gliding Club at Great Hucklow, where she piloted a glider over the village at an altitude of 2,000 feet. Some of the biggest names in show business also visited the county. Gracie Fields, already a world famous film and stage star, appeared in a concert at Derby's Grand Theatre on 13 February, and on 10 April, the actor and singer Paul Robeson appeared at the nearby Central Hall. The same venue also played host for the visit of the pianist Rubinstein. "Going to the pictures," continued as a favourite pastime as evidenced by the opening of three new cinemas – the Majestic and the Gloria in Chaddesden, and the Regal in East Street.

In August, the county itself was destined for cinematic stardom as location filming commenced for the film version of James Hilton's famous book *Goodbye Mr Chips*. Repton School played the part of Brookfields School and some 200 pupils remained at the school to appear as extras in the film.

A modern town

DERBY was boldly transforming itself into a modern, 20th-century town. On 4 February, the Princess Royal opened the new King George V Memorial Ward at the Children's Hospital on North Street. The extension, which cost £5,000, provided 21 new beds and a new operating theatre. On 30 June, Lord Herbert Scott, chairman of the directors of Rolls-Royce, opened the new £12,000 pavilion

Another 'Sam' carton from the Derby Evening Telegraph, *September 1939.*

on the works' sports ground. The same day, the Corporation's new refuse disposal plant in Stores Road, capable of handling 80 to 100 tons of waste per eight-hour day, went on-line.

In mid July, 100,000 tons of limestone was blasted from the face of Caldon Low quarries near Ashbourne. Lord Stamp, president of the LMS Railway Company, who pressed a button in his office at Euston Station, triggered the explosion. The stone was to be used in the foundations of new station buildings there.

On 22 July, Leslie Burgin, Minister of Transport, witnessed by 150 guests brought in by train from London, officially opened the new £50,000 Railway School of Transport on London Road. Elsewhere in Derby, Sir Walter Wormersley, MP, Assistant Postmaster General, officially opened the town's new automatic telephone exchange in Colyear Street. It had taken two years to build and the actual switchover had taken place almost three weeks earlier. The new exchange could deal with 10,000 subscribers from Derby alone.

Building on the new Council House beside the Derwent had, at last, begun. It was part of the Central Improvement Plan that had been under way for some years. The new building was to house some 465 council employees, previously accommodated in 24 separate buildings, and provide a formal meeting chamber for councillors, presently meeting at the Guildhall. In April, the Dowager Duchess of Devonshire had opened Chesterfield's new Town Hall.

More civic improvements

ON 8 September 1938, Derby saw the reopening of the newly refurbished Victorian Market Hall. The following day, Homelands School for Girls, the replacement for Central School for Girls, opened its classrooms on Village Street for the first time. Designed by the borough architect, C. H. Aslin, it cost nearly £46,000 and its staff would be responsible for the secondary education of some 490 pupils. Homelands' sister school, Parkfield Cedars had celebrated its 21st birthday in March.

Road building was another key area of improvement to town life. Traffic surveys showed that daily traffic in the town had risen by

4,000 vehicles in only three years, with St Peter's Street and Derwent Street the busiest. On 28 September, a new stretch of Derby's ring road was opened. This linked Alvaston and Chaddesden between London and Nottingham roads. The appropriately named Traffic Street in Derby was opened. Widening and reconstruction had cost £62,266, and Sir Harry Twyford, Lord Mayor of London, who was also in the county to attend the foundation stone laying of a new nurses' home at Belper, performed the official ceremony.

Death and disaster

ON 6 May, the 9th Duke of Devonshire, Victor Cavendish, had died. A former Governor-General of Canada, he was Lord Lieutenant of Derbyshire and had suffered a stroke some years earlier from which he had never recovered. His last official appearance had been at a children's party at Chatsworth in January. His son, the Marquess of Hartington, on his 43rd birthday, succeeded to the dukedom. The new Duke had served as MP for West Derbyshire and was succeeded in this role, following a by-election, by his brother-in-law. The new duke's sons, William and Andrew, continued their studies at Cambridge.

While the county mourned the Duke's passing, the large loss of life at Markham Colliery on 10 May cast a huge shadow of grief over the north of the county. Some 79 men lost their lives, and another 40 were injured, following an explosion at around 5.30am, just half an hour before the end of the night shift. Most died from carbon monoxide poisoning, others from severe burns and injuries. A charitable fund raised more than £40,000 for the widows and their 72 children. Less than 11 hours after the Markham explosion, a smaller incident on the surface of Mill Close Lead Mine at Darley Dale, resulted in the deaths of three men.

As 1938 drew to a close, the threat of war again loomed large. On 9 December, the Air Minister, Sir Kingsley Wood, made a timely visit to Rolls-Royce, very aware of the important role the Derby works would have should the nation have to take up arms once more.

AMERICA STRETCHES HER "HANDS ACROSS THE SEA" ONCE AGAIN...
ALICE-WHERE ART THOU?
OKAY, BUDDIES, ONLY ANOTHER 2999 MILES TO THE STATUE OF LIBERTY
THIS WEEKEND SHE HAS "ANNEXED" MORE TERRITORY IN BRITISH SPORT AND IS SLOWLY TAKING ALL OUR SILVERWARE AS WELL AS GOLD BULLION...
AT WIMBLEDON ON SATURDAY KAY STAMMERS HAD TO PLAY SECOND FIDDLE TO MISS MARBLE WHO IS TAKING 3 CHAMPIONSHIPS BACK TO U.S.A...
BOBBY RIGGS IS SINGLES, DOUBLES & MIXED CHAMP AND U.S.A. CREWS WON THE THAMES CUP, GRAND CHALLENGE CUP AND DIAMOND SCULLS AT HENLEY REGATTA: AND U.S.A. MARKSMEN WON THE PERSHING CUP...
POOR OLD WOODERSON BROKE THE A.A. MILE RECORD ON SATURDAY AFTERNOON, GRABBED HIS PRIZE AND STREAKED OFF BEFORE ANY AMERICANS PRESENT COULD ROB HIM..
PORTSMOUTH HAVE PLACED A STRONG GUARD OVER THE F.A. CUP...
DERBYSHIRE C.C.C. ARE BUILDING A STRONG-ROOM TO KEEP THE COUNTY CHAMPIONSHIP IN (IF THEY WIN IT)
AND HITLER IS FORTIFYING DANZIG TO PROTECT IT FROM FALLING INTO AMERICAN HANDS..(IT COST ADOLF A WEEK'S POCKET-MONEY WHEN AN AMERICAN DANCER WON A GOLD LOCKET OFF HIM..)

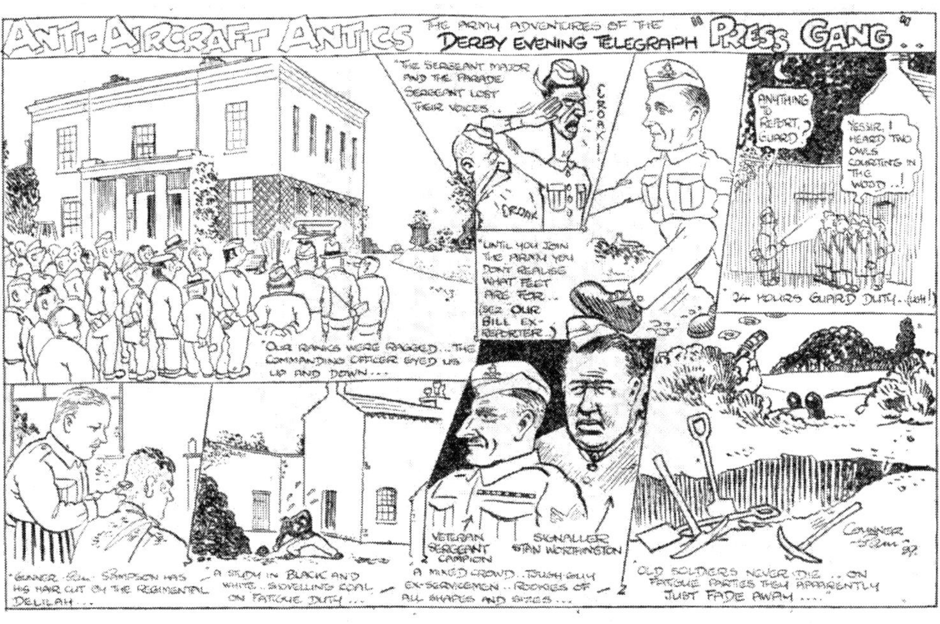
ANTI-AIRCRAFT ANTICS
THE ARMY ADVENTURES OF THE DERBY EVENING TELEGRAPH "PRESS GANG"..
THE SERGEANT MAJOR AND THE PARADE SERGEANT LOST THEIR VOICES..
CROAK!
CROAK
ANYTHING TO REPORT, GUARD?
YESSIR, I HEARD TWO OWLS COURTING IN THE WOOD..!
"UNTIL YOU JOIN THE ARMY YOU DON'T REALISE WHAT FEET ARE FOR..." SEZ "OUR BILL" EX-REPORTER..
"24 HOURS GUARD DUTY.. (UGH!)
"OUR RANKS WERE RAGGED... THE COMMANDING OFFICER EYED US UP AND DOWN...
VETERAN SERGEANT CAMPION
SIGNALLER STAN WORTHINGTON
"GUNNER BILL SAMPSON HAS HIS HAIR CUT BY THE REGIMENTAL DELILAH...
A STUDY IN BLACK AND WHITE.. SHOVELLING COAL ON FATIGUE DUTY...
A MIXED CROWD.. TOUGH-GUY EX-SERVICEMEN.. ROOKIES OF ALL SHAPES AND SIZES...
OLD SOLDIERS NEVER DIE... ON FATIGUE PARTIES THEY APPARENTLY JUST FADE AWAY...."

The War Years

Storm Clouds Gathering

TEARS steaming down the faces of his Sacheveral Street neighbours finally brought home to nine-year-old Derby boy Jim Phelps the reality of war. Until then, war had been a game played with lead soldiers and a toy cannon that fired matchsticks.

But on the morning of Sunday, 3 September 1939, Jim, a pupil at Traffic Street School, saw his mother's friends hugging and weeping. For the second time in a generation, Britain had declared war on Germany. In that moment he did a lot of growing up.

Along with the rest of the free world, Jim's hometown was destined for six years of struggle and heartbreak. Grief would touch most of its homes. There would be rationing and shortages, rumours and scares, agony and despair. Yet there would also be laughter and hope. The people of Derby who were to live through that tapestry of every human emotion starkly symbolised in the years 1939-45, would eventually agree that it was a very special time. There would be a comradeship impossible to recapture in peacetime.

But on that Sunday morning 75 years ago, there was only the shattering realisation that, for the second time in a generation, Britain was at war with Germany. The seeds had been sown in 1919, when the Treaty of Versailles imposed such swingeing punishments on a defeated Germany that the French Marshall

Foch prophetically declared: "This is not peace, it is an armistice for 20 years."

And if German remilitarisation of the Rhineland in 1936, and Hitler's annexation of Austria in 1938 could be ignored, when Germany invaded Czechoslovakia on 15 March 1939, the people of Derby surely knew that another war was inevitable.

Six months earlier, in an act of appeasement of Adolf Hitler's exploitive foreign policy, the Czech Sudetenland had been ceded to Germany. Now all the Czech people lay under Hitler's yoke. Nine days after Prague fell, Britain and France pledged to defend Belgium, Holland and Switzerland. At the end of March, Britain joined France in guaranteeing Poland's frontiers. The following day, Hitler made a violently anti-British speech. War clouds were gathering and the long summer of 1939 was one of almost unbearable tension as diplomats bluffed, bargained and threatened.

And so Derby prepared for war. By August, the town's air-raid precautions committee had delivered almost 9,000 air-raid shelters to private houses. Public shelters were adapted under railway arches in Ford Street and Lodge Lane, and in the crypt of Derby Cathedral. Trenches, each holding 740 people, were dug in Derwent, Rykneld and Osmaston recreation grounds. Passengers on Corporation buses found the windows painted blue and the internal lights now dull amber. A mock air-raid was made on the factory of Moore, Eady & Murcote Goode, near Markeaton recreation ground, and 700 workers were evacuated to the shelters.

The effectiveness of Derby's lighting blackout was tested as part of a huge ARP exercise over the southern half of Britain. Old property in Bridge Street was set alight and then dealt with by the Auxiliary Fire Service. The skies over the town throbbed to the noise of Hampden, Wellington and Blenheim bombers. In fields between Sinfin and Chellaston, a Blenheim crashed. The crew were unhurt but red red-faced as they clambered clear to explain that they had run out of fuel. The aircraft had been taking part in a huge three-day exercise in which Derbyshire was part of "Westland". To a small boy like Jim Phelps, it was all so exciting.

Council workers prepared to evacuate the municipal archives and Derby's arts treasures, while rare museum exhibits were prepared for underground storage. All manner of official leaflets appeared: "What to do on a Train Journey"; "What to do with your Pets"; "Advice to Householders taking in Unaccompanied Children".

Derby artist Ernest Townsend turned his skills to more practical use, camouflaging power station cooling towers and factories roofs.

The *Derby Evening Telegraph* carried almost daily pleas for more ARP volunteers. The town was 1,000 short of its complement, a fact underlined at Derby borough police sports day when a race for ARP messengers had to be cancelled when only one entry had been received.

August Bank Holiday weekend, 1939, saw thousands leave Derby by bus and train for what for most would be their last holiday for years. Buckets and spades were accompanied by a chilling reminder of the times – gas masks in their containers.

At Derby Racecourse on Nottingham Road, there was a three-day meeting with the legendary Gordon Richards among the jockeys. Hughie Green, to become a household name with the 1960s TV programme *Opportunity Knocks,* starred in his own show at the Grand Theatre in Babington Lane. The band of the Life Guards played to a packed Arboretum.

Towards the end of August, Derby County started a season they would never finish with a defeat at Sunderland and a win over Portsmouth at the Baseball Ground. On the cricket field, Derbyshire's George Pope was selected for an MCC tour, to India, that would never take place. Other sportsmen, too, would never fulfill their schedule. Two German cars were entered for the late September meeting at Castle Donington. One of the drivers was Manfred von Brauchitsch, a relative of a German general.

But it was war that dominated Derby's thoughts. And on Friday, 1 September, a special edition of the *Derby Evening Telegraph* carried the headline everyone had dreaded: "Poland Attacked."

Before 11am the following day, more than 2,000 children from Derby School, Kedleston Road School, Central Nursery School,

St Mary's School, Gerard Street School, Firs Estate School and Ashbourne Road School were evacuated. They included a family of six – triplets Albert, George and Gladys Ridgway (10) and their brothers Willie (13), Henry (12) and sister Constance (11) of Ponsonby Terrace.

Another 4,000 children followed over the next few days, going to places like Chesterfield, Belper, Shardlow and Ripley, where 1,000 women attended a meeting to discuss receiving Derby's evacuees.

On the Friday before war was declared, staff at Friargate station heard ticking coming from a parcel that they placed in a bucket of water. Firemen found the parcel contained several hundred pounds in cash, hundreds of pounds' worth of jewellery and a small ornamental clock. They belonged to a woman travelling from Scotland to Staffordshire.

As the last moments of peace agonisingly choked away on the hot, sultry afternoon of Saturday, 2 September, Jack Nicholas's penalty gave Derby County a 1-0 First Division win over Aston Villa at the Baseball Ground. The attendance was barely 8,000 to see the Rams' last Football League game for seven years.

That afternoon Derby's town centre was full of uniforms as soldiers, sailors and airmen mingled with housewives snapping up all remaining blackout material and first-aid requirements.

In the early evening, the streets were unusually crowded as people came out to walk and talk. Pubs everywhere were full to overflowing. Sandbagged railways stations at Derby LMS, Friargate and Nottingham Road confronted holidaymakers returning home. Over the town flew the sinister shapes of the barrage balloon defence.

Late on the very last evening of peace, Jim Phelps stood in the doorway of his mother's fish and chip shop in Sacheveral Street and watched a spectacular thunderstorm bring five balloons crashing down in flames. One fell on a power cable and plunged a large part of the town into darkness for three hours.

Jim recalled: "I went to bed on the Saturday, wondering what the morning would bring. At 11.15am we tuned in our wireless and heard the Prime Minister, Neville Chamberlain, announce that we were at war. I was so excited, I ran into the street to find my pals. Then I saw some of the neighbours. They could remember the last war. They were weeping. Suddenly I realised what it meant."

Jim spent the remainder of the day helping to fill sandbags on Burton Road. At 3.30am, the air-raid sirens sounded for Derby's first alert of the war. The Phelps family trooped to the shelter at the Unity Hall on Normanton Road. Nothing happened. It was a false alarm.

But the sirens would wail many more times. Sometimes they would herald death from the skies. The long, tense summer of 1939 was over. Derby was at war.

Communities around Derbyshire formed work parties and 6,000 volunteers registered with the Red Cross. Women began to take over the jobs of men called into the armed services. Derby's retiring mayor, Alderman D. S. Butler, declined the usual celebratory meal in view of the war and 16 members of the Town Council, who had been due to retire, remained in office without re-election under the Local Elections and Register of Electors Act of 1939.

The fear of separation for thousands of young men from their families and sweethearts saw an instant upsurge in the number of weddings. Between September and November 1939, Derby Register Office played host to some 200 marriages, three times as many as in the same three months of 1938.

The 350 "enemy aliens" registered in Derbyshire each had to appear before a tribunal in October. Most were refugees from Germany and Austria, and were treated sympathetically. Their registration cards were marked "Refugee from Nazi Oppression" and many were permitted to register for National Service or to seek employment.

EVEN during this time of great crisis, the minutiae of everyday life in Derby in 1939 continued uninterrupted. There were celebrations, of course, like those in January to mark the 80th birthday of Alderman George Wood. Regarded by many as the "father" of Derby Town Council, Alderman Wood had been a well-respected councillor for Normanton since 1905. The same month saw the opening of the new Roe Farm School in Chaddesden; in May, a celebratory luncheon was held in Derby to mark the jubilee of Derbyshire County Council.

Later in 1939, two new churches – the Baptist Church on Broadway and St Edmund's Church at Allenton – welcomed their first congregations, in September and December respectively. On a sadder note, 1939 saw the deaths of two men with widely differing backgrounds, both of whom were hugely respected in their own way. Thomas Stevens, who died on 20 February, was an octogenarian who held the distinction of having worked longer for the same employer than any other man in Derbyshire. During his 71 years with the Derby firm of F. Longdon & Co, Mr Stevens had never been late for work and had rarely taken a day off through illness.

On 17 July, Derby mourned the death of Dr Henry Howe Bemrose. A former mayor and member of the Town Council for 35 years, Alderman Bemrose had been Derbyshire's Boy Scouts commissioner since 1923 and chairman of the Education Committee for 15 years. In 1930, Bemrose School on Uttoxeter Road had been named in his honour.

As the situation in Europe grew ever more serious, local events took on a military flavour. The date 12 March marked the beginning of National Service Week when a parade of 500 members of various military units, and a service at Derby Cathedral were held – all part of encouraging the local population to volunteer.

In June, Sir Kingsley Wood, the Air Minister, officially opened the Corporation Airport at Burnaston. Thousands of Derbyshire folk attending were entertained by a display from the RAF and Fleet Air Arm. Soon, however, Derby Airport would be on a war footing.

A Phoney War

SOME called it the Phoney War, others the Twilight War. But whatever title you cared to give it, life in Derby had an almost surreal quality during the first few months of the Second World War. Everyone knew it would be different once it all began, and it was – but different in an entirely unexpected way.

People expected Neville Chamberlain's announcement to be followed by wave after wave of German bombers. They had seen cinema newsreel of what had happened to the Poles. But nothing happened.

There were no air-raids, no bombs and no drastic changes between the state of war which now existed and the state of emergency which had lasted all summer.

The warning siren that had sent Derby's citizens scurrying to their shelters on the first night of the war had been a precaution until aircraft over the eastern counties had been identified. The first enemy aircraft did not arrive in the vicinity until early December, when a Heinkel reconnaissance was spotted.

In reality, Hitler was hoping that, after he had smashed Poland, Britain and her allies would sue for peace. Initially he forbade air attacks on British towns and cities. The appalling European winter of 1939-40 meant a further delay.

German reticence did not extend to the sea, however. At 9pm on the first day of the war, the British liner *Athenia*, bound for Montreal, was sunk by a German submarine 250 miles off the Hebrides. The Germans claimed that she had been mistaken for an armed merchant vessel. The death toll of 112 included 28 Americans. Among the 1,000 passengers rescued was a Derby couple, Mr and Mrs Graham Hopkinson, who spent nine hours in an open boat before being picked up by a Norwegian steamer and landed at Galway in southern Ireland.

But that aside, life went on pretty much as normal. True, posters everywhere exhorted the people of Derby to "Carry your gas mask at all times, " but there was no apparent danger, and no food shortages either. The *Derby Evening Telegraph* carried advertisements for whisky, meat, radios and furniture, and there were plenty of fresh vegetables. New potatoes were selling for one old penny per pound, and cauliflowers at twopence each. There were even plenty of oranges at threepence each.

There was also plenty to grumble about. Everyone had braced themselves for the bombing of innocent civilians, but the last few months of 1939 were an anticlimax. Derby's attitude was typical of the whole country: we'll face up to whatever Hitler might throw at us, but there is no danger and all we can see is a lot of tiresome, petty regulations.

One restriction that affected everybody was the blackout. Total blackout was the order and the cry "Put that light out!" had people hastily checking their own arrangements in case a small chink of light had escaped into the inky night. Derby borough magistrates threatened to get tough with so-called "lighting offenders", as dozens of otherwise law-abiding citizens found themselves hauled in front of the courts.

Getting about in the blackout was a serious problem. Street lamps were switched off and torches were in short supply. People fumbled about in the dark, apologising to lamp posts and pillar boxes.

Dangerous driving conditions caused by the blackout saw fatal road accidents double in the last four months of 1939. In September alone, 20 people lost their lives on Derby's roads, against only six in 1938. The comment was made, more than once, that Hitler appeared to be killing his enemies without the need for air-raids. He just persuaded them to turn off all the lights. In February 1940, the Government introduced a 20mph speed limit during the blackout, and Double Summer Time gave travellers another hour of daylight travel in the early evening.

The issue of gas masks was another irritation that Derby people accepted, although a spot check revealed that many people used the containers to carry their lunchtime sandwiches. The absence of bombing also saw the return to Derby of many of the children who had been evacuated. Parents missed their children, the kids were homesick, and there was no sign of danger. It seemed a pointless heartache.

A few Derby men became the object of their neighbours' scorn when they refused to be called-up for military service. As the list of reserved occupations was continually modified, and more and more men became eligible for call-up, so the number of conscientious objectors grew. Tribunals were set up to deal with their cases, although the number of hearings reported in the *Derby Evening Telegraph* in the early months of the war indicated that there was little consistency in their verdicts. Sometimes a man was deemed a genuine objector, sometimes not.

One young man in Gerard Street hit upon the idea of ingesting large quantities of scalding hot tea with bread and dripping immediately before his army medical. His hopes that this would somehow render him unfit for military service were soon dashed and he then became a conscientious objector on religious grounds, which worked.

As Derby's first Christmas of the war approached and shops became busier, it seemed like any pre-war Christmas. Ranby's Toytown offered "a good selection of toys". The Central Educational suggested gas mask containers in its guide to last-minute shopping. Opticians Lancaster & Thorpe advertised Polaroid spectacles for motorists, while Joe Simpson's pawnshop on London Road offered "highest prices paid" for false teeth.

Cinemas, which had re-opened in September after being closed for a few days while the Government decided on its policy concerning places of entertainment, stayed open on Christmas Day and there were queues outside many. Six hundred Derbeians attended a midnight dance at the Plaza Ballroom, dancing until 3am on Christmas morning. At the Tudor Ballroom in Abbey Street, people danced to the Manhatten Band.

At the Grand Theatre in Babington Lane, the pantomime *Goldilocks and the Three Bears* played to packed houses. Hotels – the Royal, the Midland and the Friary – were all booked to capacity.

On Christmas morning 1939, Derby Corinthians met Old Bemrosians at Alvaston in a football match to raise money for the Red Cross. In the Corinthians' line-up was a tiny winger, Reg Harrison. Just over six years later he would collect an FA Cup winners' medal as a member of Derby County's winning Wembley team.

When the Mayor of Derby, Alderman A. Neal, visited 3 Boundary Road on Christmas Day, he was shown a congratulatory telegram sent by King George VI to Mr and Mrs Joseph Ingram, who were celebrating their 60th wedding anniversary.

Ten years behind the Ingrams were Mr and Mrs William Lawton of 133 Gerard Street. On that first Christmas Day of the war, they celebrated their 50th wedding anniversary with a small family party.

Local families opened their homes to servicemen stationed near Derby, themselves far from home. At the LMS station on Christmas night, there were warm embraces as some troops left, their leave over; and joyful reunions as others arrived, their break from duty about to begin.

On the wireless, the King gave his famous Christmas message, "I said to the man who stood at the gate of the year…" while a NAAFi concert featured Gracie Fields from "somewhere in France".

"Somewhere in England" was Una Roe, who had given up her dance studio in Derby to go on the stage with Tex Osborne, a cowboy rope expert. Una played the piano accordion while Tex spun his rope. At Christmas 1939, their act, Tex and Una, was entertaining troops at an unnamed barracks.

Perish the thought, but the nearest first-class football for those fans suffering withdrawal symptoms at the closure of the Baseball Ground was at Nottingham, where Forest and County were due to play in a regional league match.

And so the minutiae of life in wartime Derby carried on. As the *Derby Evening Telegraph* of December 27, 1939, put it. "It is hard to realise that there is a war on." All that was about to change. The anticlimax was about to end. In 1940, the people of Derby would begin to discover that life was going to be different after all.

"Look, Duck and Vanish ..."

IT was the day that the people of Derby knew the Phoney War was over. The front-page headline in the *Derby Evening Telegraph* of 10 May 1940, told them the worst – Germany had invaded the Low Countries. Geography had placed Belgium, Holland and Luxembourg in Hitler's path. News that German paratroopers had landed there, and that tanks were rolling across their borders, now brought the war very much closer to Derby.

Until April, when Germany invaded Denmark and Norway, it had been a war fought exclusively in the east. In just one day in May, however, it was raging just across the English Channel. All the preparations and restrictions that had dominated the lives of

Members of the newly formed Home Guard watch a demonstration of musketry drill during a training course at Kingsway in August 1940.

Derby people for the previous eight months took on a sinister new significance.

For one Derby man in particular, the Germans' lightning swoop into Belgium heralded days of danger and hair-raising adventure.

Dundonald Jackson's home was in Swinburne Street, Derby. Usually, his routine might have involved a stroll into town down Babington Lane. In May 1940, however, Mr Jackson was a Rolls-Royce service engineer in Belgium. On the day of the German invasion, he waited until nightfall before making a dash for safety with his wife and personal assistant. Along the road leading to the Belgian coast they passed hundreds of British soldiers moving up the front line. On one occasion they were forced to abandon their car and take refuge in a ditch as a German fighter aircraft machine-gunned the road.

Eventually they were able to board a Belgian steamer jammed full of refugees. Again they were straffed by the Luftwaffe. After a perilous journey across the Channel they landed in England and made their way home to Derby, to a town still recovering from the realisation that the invasion of Britain was now a very real possibility.

The Jacksons also found that Britain had a new Prime Minister. With the German invasion of the Low Countries, Winston Churchill had replaced Neville Chamberlain at the head of a Coalition Government.

Along with the rest of the nation, Derbeians tuned into their wireless sets to be told that the new Premier could offer them only "blood, sweat, tears and toil".

Derby's emergency services were ready for whatever Mr Churchill promised. Some 3,000 volunteers took part in a major ARP exercise. The town suffered "heavy damage and scores of casualties" during a mock air-raid. And the people of Derby were given a timely reminder of the horrors they might face when yellow smoke, simulating a poison gas attack, curled into the air between St Mary's Gate and Walker Lane. Derby's shops, offices and schools remained open over the Whitsuntide holiday, but housewives found it difficult to buy meat

On 15 May 1940, the Secretary of State for War, Anthony Eden, announced the formation of the Local Defence Volunteers. Originally dubbed "Look, Duck and Vanish", the LDV were later renamed the Home Guard, to be immortalised 25 years later by the BBC television series *Dad's Army*. Their prime function was to guard key installations and oppose German airborne landings until regular troops could be deployed. Later they manned anti-aircraft rocket batteries.

Derby's men were quick to come forward. On the first day, 450 volunteered; at the end of the first week, that number had climbed to more than 1,000. One of the first to enlist in the new force was Alec McWilliams, who went on to become a director of Rolls-Royce before his death in the 1990s. He became a lieutenant in the R-R unit and recalled: "At first we were equipped with LDV armbands, and later with denim boiler suits. We had to find our own weapons and, in the early stages, these ranged from rifles and pistols to pitchforks and pikestaffs. Our first role was as an anti-sabotage unit. When the sirens sounded and the factory was deserted, the authorities felt that we were open to someone either planting a bomb, or doing some crude sabotage like placing a spoke in one of the machines.

"As time wore on, we were renamed the Home Guard and were given proper uniforms and weapons, like rifles and Thompson sub-machine guns. Looking back, people were more objective during the war and there wasn't time to indulge in petty differences."

Lew Patrick, who lived in Harcourt Street, reported to his Home Guard unit at Kingsway Drill Hall after working 12-hour shifts at the Carriage and Wagon Works. Lew recalled: "In those days, you never counted the hours or watched the clock. If a job needed doing, you just got on with it. It was nothing to spend 12 hours in a factory and then report for Home Guard duty. Then a few hours sleep and back to work."

Derby's Home Guard were just some of the 1.6 million men who served until late in 1944, when the Government disbanded the force after the Allied landings on D-Day.

In Derby in 1940, however, people began to prepare for a long war. The *Derby Evening Telegraph* joined forces with the Derby

Sherwood Foresters, recently returned from Dunkirk, outside the LMS station in June 1940.

Soldiers line up for inspection outside the LMS railway station in 1940.

Gas, Light and Coke Company to arrange a series of lectures entitled "Economic Wartime Cookery" given by Beryl Abbey at the Temperance Hall in Curzon Street.

The threat of invasion also brought the inevitable rumours. Chaddesden Parish Council called upon Derbyshire's chief constable to investigate reports that aliens in Chaddesden had been passing information to the Germans. Rolls-Royce Thrift Society found it necessary to post notices denying a rumour that the Government would confiscate any cash left in their accounts by 1 June.

At the Merchant Hall, a meeting of 500 men from Derby's Carriage and Wagon Works heard that they faced redundancy because of a shortage of timber after the fall of Norway. Even going to the pictures was affected. Derby Town Council refused to allow the town's cinemas to open on Sundays because staff shortages meant that safety regulations could not be implemented.

On 28 May, the Allies were struck a devastating blow. The Belgian government capitulated and left soldiers of the British Expeditionary Force exposed to the might of Hitler's war machine as it swept on towards France. "Dunkirk not yet menaced," said the following day's *Derby Evening Telegraph* headline. But a few days later, Derby's LMS station saw the arrival of 6,000 men, some of the remnants of the BEF, still wearing the uniforms in which they had been plucked out of the sea off the French port whose name would become one of the most powerful symbols of the Second World War.

Alf Turner, an engineer at Rolls-Royce, remembered seeing many of the survivors standing in London Road. "They looked lost, absolutely lost. It made us realise that we weren't invincible."

On 31 May, Derby's borough surveyor's department began moving all road signs in the town. Work began on the ring-road, and by midday the battery of signs at the top of the Cornmarket had disappeared.

Nameplates on all of Derby's railway stations were removed, and the destination boards on all Trent buses disappeared. Conductors were ordered not to call out the names of stops.

There were plans to build a 600-bed emergency hospital on land adjoining the City Hospital, and on 1 June soldiers helped firemen fight a blaze which partially destroyed a stand at Derby Racecourse. Bizarrely, Brussel sprouts were growing in the flowerbeds at the Arboretum.

In August, 100 German and Austrian women, some of the nuns, were arrested and brought to Derby to board a train which would take to them on the first part of their journey to internment on the Isle of Man. Concrete tank barriers and pill boxes – many of them still evident in the countryside around Derby today – were erected, and in the Doveridge area, locals discovered German parachute harnesses. They turned out to be an attempt by the Nazis to create local panic.

On Thursday, 8 August 1940, the people of Derby awoke to learn that they had special visitors: the King and Queen were coming to town.

The fact that the Royal couple was to tour Rolls-Royce – where the Merlin engines which powered Britain's hopes in the imminent Battle of Britain were manufactured – meant that their visit had to remain secret until the last possible moment. But word somehow

The King and Queen visit Roll-Royce in August 1940.

King George VI inspects Indian troops stationed at Osmaston polo grounds in August 1940.

got out and thousands were waiting at the LMS station when King George VI and Queen Elizabeth arrived.

The King, wearing the uniform of colonel-in-chief of the Grenadier Guards, was told by Derby's mayor, Alderman Arthur Neal: "You will find your citizens here as loyal as any in the British Empire."

After inspecting Indian mounted troops stationed at Osmaston polo grounds, the King and Queen walked through the Rolls-Royce factory at Nightingale Road, where journalists and photographers were excluded from the experimental department. Then, after meeting First World War VC, Charles Stone, stroking the factory cat and appearing on a balcony to wave to workers, they returned to the railway station, leaving Derby to get on with its war.

The War on Our Doorsteps

ALTHOUGH he still lived in Wilmorton's Ellesmere Avenue, Fred Gifford was constantly in the front line of the war in 1941. As a station officer in Derby's Auxiliary Fire Service, Mr Gifford nightly found himself defying bombs and falling buildings as he helped to fight fires at the height of the blitz. And on the nights when Derby itself escaped the bombing, there was no respite for Mr Gifford and his colleagues.

As the Luftwaffe rained death upon British cities, the AFS would be rushed to Birmingham, Leicester, Liverpool, London, and even Belfast, to tackle frightening blazes. On one occasion, AFS men from Derby fought oil fires at Thameshaven for three days without respite.

Before he died in August 1979, primarily as a result of the conditions he had endured during the war, Mr Gifford recalled those dreadful days: "Often we'd arrive in a town as complete strangers

These houses in Kendon Avenue, Sunnyhill, escaped with only minor damage after Derby's first air-raid of the Second World War, in June 1940.

and be directed to our own particular fire through streets ablaze on either side. Then we had to find the nearest water supply and get on with the job. Twelve-hour shifts were a nightly occurrence and map reading was essential, because all the road signs had been removed in case of an invasion. It was very hairy. Often we'd fight fires with bombs falling all around us.

"There were lighter moments, of course. Before the war I was the signalling examiner for the Boy Scouts and, using the boys who had passed the test, I evolved a scheme for a chain of communication of visual signalling from Jury Street to the outer fire stations. Using the Cathedral tower, we were able to make contact with all the stations with Morse code and flags. It caused a sensation and one day the trapdoor opened and a policeman stuck his head through and asked: 'What's going on here?'

"With the co-operation of the Sherwood Foresters stationed on Markeaton Park, and using their daylight signalling equipment, we enlarged the scheme. But we could only loan the Foresters' equipment, so Station Officer Raynor and I experimented with

A police officer inspects damage to the house in Jackson Avenue, Mickleover, where Mrs Elsie Hanson was fatally injured in the first air-raid of the Second World War on Derby, in June 1940.

Houses in Regent Street were destroyed in the air-raid of August 20, 1940.

car sidelights and batteries. It was never used, but the number of times we were reported for 'signalling to the enemy' was amazing."
By comparison with other cities, Derby escaped lightly at the height of the blitz. But there were still enough raids to cause havoc and heartache to many people. The first bombs fell on Derby on the night of 25 June 1940. Two houses in Jackson Avenue, Mickleover, were destroyed. Mrs Elsie Henson, aged 39, whose parents lived in Shepherd Street, Littleover, was hit in the head, chest and legs by splinters when a bomb fell in a neighbouring garden as she tried to enter her air-raid shelter. She died of her injuries in Derby City Hospital, six days after the raid. Derby's first air-raid casualty had been 67-year-old Elizabeth Evans, who died at her home in Violet Street on the 25th itself.

By August 1940, the air-raid sirens were sounding almost nightly and police had to prevent frightened Derbeians from camping out in their shelters. On 14 August, Margaret Hutton was killed at her

Derby LMS railway station repaired after being damaged in an air-raid in January 1941.

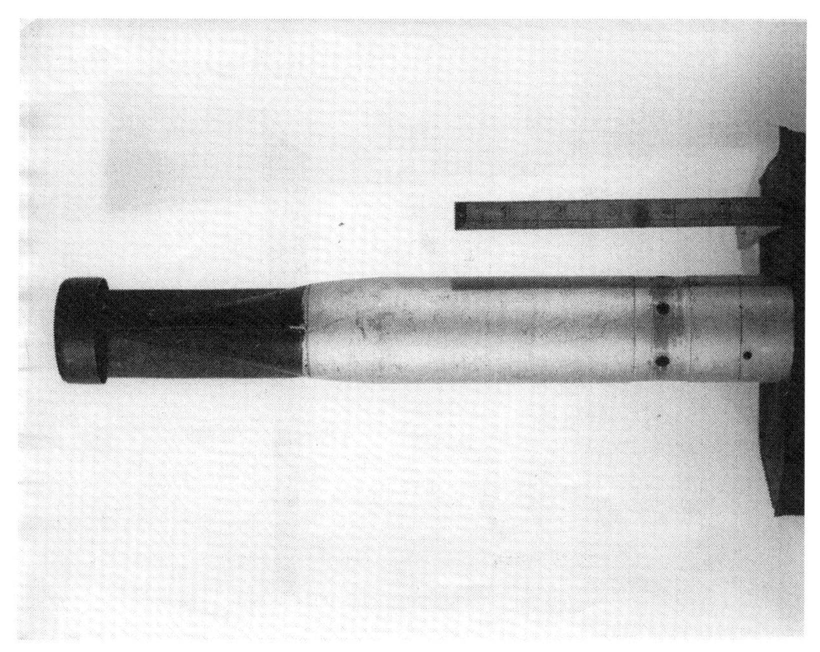

This incendiary bomb failed to go off after being dropped during a raid over Derbyshire in September 1940.

Damage to property in Offerton Avenue, Derby, during an air-raid in January 1941.

home in Hawthorn Street; an overnight four-hour raid on 19-20 August left three dead: Annie Andrews of Litchurch Street died on her way to the nearby Derbyshire Royal Infimary; Doris Bentley and her daughter Sheila, both of Regent Street, died in hospital the day after the raid.

The *Derby Evening Telegraph* could only report of an air-raid "on a Midlands town" and a photograph of the bomb-damaged Osmaston Stand at the Baseball Ground was described simply as "a famous Midlands football ground".

Giant oil burners that belched foul smoke were used to mask the town from the air, as Derbeians heard German bombers droning overhead towards Sheffield and Manchester. Alex McWilliams recalled standing on high ground at Littleover and seeing the south-western sky red as blood as fires raged in Birmingham and Coventry.

The bandstand at the Arboretum, mangled after being hit by a German bomb in January 1941.

On the night of 15 January 1941, Derby suffered its heaviest raid of the war. Fifty high-explosive bombs fell on the town, killing 20 civilians, injuring 48 others and damaging or destroying 1,650 houses.

There were two alerts, the first from 9pm to 1.17am; the second from 3.15am to 5.20am. Extensive damage was done to the LMS Station, where a dozen bombs fell. Some of them failed to explode but others brought down the roof, while the bridge connecting the platform crashed down completely blocking the lines.

A wall collapsed, killing Arthur Hallowes of Breaston and his near-neighbour, Cecil Purser, a member of the Home Guard. Also killed that night were Harry Smith of Chaddesden, and two Bolton men, Chris Snailham and Vic Rutherford, along with several soldiers. Seven months later, another body was discovered under the rubble.

Six people died at the Park Gates on London Road: Margaret Jackson 43; Ruby Priestly and Ron Rowland, both 18; Arthur Watts 27; and Gwen Young, 21. Edna Payne, 20, died next day at the Derbyshire Royal Infirmary

Another six perished when bombs fell in the Cavendish area: Gladys Foss and her husband, Sid, and mother and daughter Elsie

Derby Lane and Kenilworth Avenue both suffered significant bomb damage.

and Christine Jones, died in hospital after their house in Kenilworth Avenue was hit; at Offerton Avenue, Rachel Percival and her daughter, Brenda, were killed.

The final victim of that 1941 raid was Florence Brewster, who died in hospital after being critically injured at her home in Madeley Street.

Two later victims that year were ARP warden Thomas Fitzgerald, who was killed outside his Shelton Lock home in May, and Arthur Adamson, who died at the Carriage and Wagon Works in July.

Of the January raid, Fred Gifford recalled: "We had to rope off our own street, Ellesmere Avenue, because it was thought that an unexploded bomb was in the road. It turned out to be a railway buffer that had been blown there after bomb had fallen on the line."

The same month, fire watching became a nightly vigil for many people and works buildings were to be manned for the next three and a half years until the danger was considered past. By the middle of March 1941, Derby had more than 15,000 supplementary firefighters, and preparations to deal with the town's homeless were speeded up in the event of air-raids on the scale that Coventry was suffering. Some 30 emergency feeding and rest centres provided accommodation for 5,000 people. Run by voluntary workers, they were equipped with palliasses, blankets, crockery and cooking utensils, portable boilers, large food stocks and baby feeding bottles.

Extravagant German claims were made for the "plastering" of Rolls-Royce – which, as we shall, was hit only once – and many bombs meant for Derby were dropped over a wider area. A mother and her daughter were killed at Long Eaton, and ten people died when a lone bomber ditched his load over Melbourne.

Although bombs did not follow many of the 148 alerts, Derby was still hit by 152 high-explosive bombs and 164 incendiaries, which killed 74 people and injured more than 300. Between 3,000 and 4,000 houses were damaged or destroyed and no lists of victims could be published at the time. It would be half a century before the civilian casualties of Derby's war were finally commemorated on the city's war memorial.

Servicemen entering the Baseball Ground on the eve of the Second World War.

The Rams at War

THERE was a strangely unreal atmosphere for Derby County's First Division match against Aston Villa at the Baseball Ground on Saturday, 2 September 2, 1939. Barely 8,000 Rams supporters bothered to attend, and as they trudged away on a stifling afternoon, few were discussing their team's 1-0 victory. It was to be the last time they would see the Rams in League action for seven years as top-flight football closed down for the duration of the Second World War.

Derby County had started that 1939-40 season reasonably well. After a 3-0 defeat at Sunderland on the opening day, they had beaten Portsmouth 2-0 on the following Wednesday before 10,000 spectators. Then Villa were beaten, and in all other circumstances supporters had every reason to look forward to the following nine months.

But even as they made their way towards the Baseball Ground for that afternoon's match, Derby's fans knew that, whatever the result, it would probably count for nothing. They saw skipper Jack Nicholas score the only goal of the game from the penalty spot after Scottish international centre-forward Dave McCulloch had been fouled. Their minds, though, were on events in Europe.

The previous day, Hitler had invaded Poland and it was highly unlikely that he would heed British demands to withdraw. The country stood on the brink of war. Football was an irrelevance as the last hours of peace choked away on that sultry afternoon.

Derby fielded two new players that day. Outside-right Wilf Walsh had signed from Arsenal, for £2,000, and his inside-right partner, Wilf Redfern, had joined the Rams from Luton Town, with Reg Stockill going in the other direction as part of the deal. The newcomers' part in Derby County's history was to be fleeting to say the least.

The Rams team for that last peacetime game was: Boulton; Wilcox, Howe; Nicholas, Barker, Ward; Walsh, Redfern, McCulloch, Stamps, Duncan.

That night most of the players gathered at the Anglers' Arms in Spondon, to discuss what might happen to them in the coming months. About one thing they were fairly sure: football would play only a small part in their lives, if indeed it featured at all.

The following morning, Sunday, September 3, along with the rest of Britain they gathered around their wireless sets to hear Prime Minister Neville Chamberlain announce that Hitler had given no undertaking to withdraw from Poland and that "consequently, this country is at war with Germany".

The Football League announced immediately that the season had been abandoned. Results counted for nothing, the games played and the goals scored would never figure in players' career records.

Within a few days, however, the League published its ideas for wartime regional competitions, with clubs allowed to field guest players, thus giving opportunities for footballers serving in the military to play for a club near to where they were stationed.

On September 30, to test public opinion, the Rams met Leeds United in a friendly at the Baseball Ground. When only 1,805 paying customers turned up to see Derby lose 3-1, the Derby board decided that wartime football was not for them and closed the club down, for the duration they said.

Some Rams players decamped 16 miles up the road to guest for Notts County, who had decided to continue. Some went down to the Assembly Rooms in Derby Market Place to enlist in the services. The rest found war work in local factories.

The Baseball Ground, meanwhile, was given over to the military and the Ordnance Corps moved in. The following year, when the Local Defence Volunteers – later the Home Guard – was formed, the Rams pitch, now overgrown, saw members of Dad's Army drilling on it. Derby's players, meanwhile, were spread far and wide as they waited to be posted overseas. Dave McCulloch guested for

Home Guard recruits doing PT exercises on an already overgrown Baseball Ground pitch in September 1940.

Bath City, Tim Ward, assigned to 153 Field Ambulance of the 15th Scottish Division, found himself playing for Hamilton Academical. Jack Stamps joined the Royal Artillery and was soon in France as a member of the British Expeditionary Force.

In June 1940, Stamps was one of the last British soldiers to be lifted off the beaches at Dunkirk after the Germans had overrun the Low Countries. After waiting for hours waist deep in the sea, he went to board a small boat. An officer pointed a pistol at him: "Soldier, if you try to board, I will shoot you, make no mistake."

"Please yourself," said the burly Rams forward, hauling himself aboard, "because if you don't, the Germans will."

The officer thought twice and six years later Jack Stamps was a hero of a different kind, with two goals for Derby County in an FA Cup Final.

A few players stayed in Derby, working in reserved occupations, Ralph Hann, Dally Duncan and Jack Bowers helping the Carriage and Wagon Works to have the best football team in their history.

Meanwhile, Derby County was involved in a crisis unconnected with the war. In August 1941, a joint FA-League commission sitting at the Midland Hotel, suspended several officials *sine die* and fined the club £500 after all manner of financial irregularities had been discovered in the club's accounts. Illegal payments to players in the late 1930s had been balanced by some inventive bookkeeping such as paying "phantom" groundsmen and claiming for journeys that were never made.

On Christmas Day, 1941, Derby County returned to the Baseball Ground with a game against the RAF. A crowd of 10,000 saw the Rams lose 3-1, but making his debut was a 16-year-old Bemrose School boy. Tommy Powell would go on to make over 400 appearances for the Rams in peacetime.

Also playing that day were two young amateurs, Jack Parr and Chick Musson. Parr would miss the 1946 Cup Final with a broken arm, but Musson would collect a winner's medal that day.

That truncated 1941-42 season saw the Rams play friendlies against teams as diverse as Birmingham, Anti-Aircraft Command, a British Army XI, the Pick of the Derby & District Senior League, the Belgian Army and the Czechoslovakian Armed Forces. They beat the Czechs 11-4, so there was no shortage of entertainment.

In July 1942, a former Rams player, Arthur "Rasher" Bacon, was one of more than 20 fatalities when a lone Dornier attacked the Rolls-Royce works at Nightingale Road. He was on duty as a special policeman.

In January 1941, the Baseball Ground itself had been a casualty with the Osmaston Stand badly damaged by German bombs.

In 1942-43, the Rams joined the Football League North and competitive football returned. With team selection a lottery, however, there were some bizarre results. Derby opened with a 6-1 win at Notts County, lost 8-1 at Wolves in November, and two months later beat Mansfield Town 10-0.

In the latter game, Leon Leuty made his debut. A pre-war Rams amateur, Leuty had been guesting for Notts County and playing for Derby Corinthians and Rolls-Royce, where he worked. One of Leuty's team-mates at Corinthians was Reg Harrison. Both Leuty and Harrison were also to collect FA Cup winner's medals when peacetime football resumed.

A lot depended on who was on leave and who was stationed nearby. Defender Jack Nicholas – who had taken over the running of the team after pre-war manager George Jobey was one of those suspended for making illegal payments – had to play in goal at Barnsley in September 1944. First-choice Frank Boulton was stranded in Birmingham and his replacement arrived at Derby Bus Station a few minutes after the Rams' transport had left.

In March 1944, Derby made a proper appointment when former Huddersfield Town manager Ted Magner became their new manager. Under Magner, the Rams won the Midland Cup in 1945, beating Aston Villa over two legs, in the second of which Peter Doherty scored five times. Two years later, Doherty, and another guest player from the RAF, Raich Carter, were to inspire the Rams' Wembley win and give their names to a short but hugely significant era in Derby County's history.

On May 9, 1945, with the war in Europe at an end, the Rams met Nottingham Forest in victory celebration match at the Baseball

Ground, where 6,901 spectators saw two goals from Doherty gives Derby a 2-2 draw.

The same month, a Horsley Woodhouse coal merchant was fined £1 10s (£1.50) plus costs by Derby magistrates for "misuse of petrol". His crime? He had driven his son to the Baseball Ground to watch the Rams.

In August 1945, the Rams met Forest at the City Ground in another celebration match, this time to mark VJ Day and the end of the war in the Far East. Derby won 4-1.

Over the August Bank Holiday weekend, Derby County had visited war-ravaged Germany to play two games, against the 83rd Group (won 10-4) and 8th Corps (lost 1-0). The Rams paid their own expenses and played to crowds of 5,000 servicemen, some of whom had worked overnight to fill in a bomb crater near one corner-flag at Keil Stadium, so that the second game could go ahead.

Football still had some way to go, but the Rams were back.

The Rams team which beat Nottingham Forest 5-0 at the Baseball Ground in September 1944. Back row (left to right): John Marshall, Reg Trim, Jimmy Bullions, Ray Bilton, Leon Leuty, Chick Musson. Front row: Peter Doherty, Sammy Crooks, Fred Tapping, Tommy Powell, Dally Duncan.

The Day They Bombed Rolls-Royce

IT is the greatest myth of Derby in the Second World War – the day they bombed Rolls-Royce. The story goes something like this: a daring lone Dornier 217, piloted by a former Rolls-Royce worker, attacks the R-R works at low-level, drops some bombs, machine-guns workers who are changing shifts, and then goes on a shooting spree around the town before heading for the coast, where it is shot down over the North Sea.

Rolls-Royce was indeed hit during the war – and by a low-flying Dornier 217 – but the rest is folklore, embellished over decades by locals confused by several issues on that chaotic morning over 70 years ago.

The nearest anyone will now ever get to the truth of what happened on the drizzly, murky day of 27 July 1942, is the meticulously-researched account by two Derby men – Peter Felix and Peter Kirk – both members of the Derbyshire Historical Aviation Society. Their detective work, carried out over many years, drew the inescapable conclusion that there were two German bombers over Derby that day. One carried out the famous raid on Rolls-Royce; the other just happened to be passing, probably on its way back from a successful raid on a northern city, and "shot-up" the town while still on a high.

It has long been a puzzle as to why Rolls-Royce's Derby works, where the Merlin aero-engine was manufactured, escaped so lightly during the Second World War. Simple geography is one answer; Derby is fairly low-lying. The town's wartime smokescreens is another. But one myth that can be debunked is that the British could somehow "bend" the Germans' navigational beams and send the Luftwaffe to other cities instead. It was possible to jam both the *X-Verfahren* and *Knickebein* beams, but not to bend them.

The answer is much more simple. Decent anti-aircraft defences and several strokes of good fortune is the probable answer to why

Rolls-Royce largely got away with it. By late 1940, Derby was defended by 28 3.7mm AA guns, which were stationed on sites like the Racecourse and Markeaton Park, and by eight Bofors and 26 Lewis machine-guns. In addition some 30 barrage balloon flew over the town.

The Germans had tried to hit Rolls-Royce often enough. On 19-20 August 1940, the Luftwaffe set out to bomb the factory but instead hit Ley's, the railway lines and several nearby houses. The following night they tried again, and once more were unsuccessful.

On 29 September they came back again, and yet again on 2 October. On the latter occasion, a Heinkel dropped its bombs on Stanton Ironworks. The aircraft was shot down off the Lincolnshire coast, an incident that later gave rise to the myth that the lone Dornier of July 1942 had been brought down on its way home.

On the night of 15-16 January 1941, Derby suffered its heaviest raid of the war when the LMS station was hit along with several houses in Normanton and on London Road, as well as Bliss's factory on City Road. Again, Royce's escaped.

There were two more attempts that year – in February and May – before the morning of 27 July 1942, when Dornier U5+LS took off from Deelen airfield, north of Arnhem. It was the 11th mission for the four-man crew: Helmut Ueberson (pilot); Kurt Kuhling (navigator); Josef Kong (flight engineer); and Gunter Bartnik (wireless operator).

One of several bombers, each with a specific target over a wide area of northern England, Ueberson's Dornier crossed the east coast over the Wash before approaching Derby from the south.

Ueberson later broadcast his account of the raid to the German armed forces: "My objective was the Rolls-Royce factory at Derby. I started at 6am and crossed the North Sea at low altitude with another of our planes. We separated near the British coast and I made for my target. The weather was bad. Suddenly I saw an airfield [*near Grantham*]. I couldn't avoid it, so I increased my speed and roared right over it. My front gunner fired at the enemy hanger.

"We continued just below the clouds, and soon found the railway which we had been told to look out for. We followed it

RE/B13/10/2

CONFIDENTIAL

VISIT TO ROLLS ROYCE DERBY

The Rolls Royce Works at Derby were bombed at 8.16 a.m. on the 27th July. A visit was paid to the works to get a preliminary statement from the management about the effects of the raid, pending the preparation of a full report by R.E. Department, Ministry of Home Security.

The attack was made by a single aircraft, which dropped four bombs estimated at 500 kilogrammes weight. The last bomb in the stick fell on the raw material stores at the extreme edge of the factory area. The remaining three bombs fell among housing outside the works. Twelve of Rolls Royce employees were killed, about half of them in the factory grounds, and the others in their homes. The bomb which fell on the stores practically destroyed the building, which is about 200 feet by 70 feet, removed half the roof sheeting from the adjacent automatic machine tool shop, and seriously weakened the roof of the forge which is adjacent to the stores. In the stores building itself, one reeling machine was completely destroyed and some power saws were damaged. Racks of small gear were overturned and the contents scattered and a number of records were destroyed. The principal contents of the stores, which are billets of alloy steel, steel rods, etc., were unaffected.

The automatic machine shop was shut down for three days and nights while the roof was repaired. The forge was shut down for about the same length of time, and it is possible it may have to be shut down for a further week while the damaged roof is put right.

The management, as far as they can see at present, do not expect to lose any production of engines as a result of the raid. In most classes of output from the automatic machine shop there were sufficient stocks to carry on, although one or two items had to be transferred to other machines to avoid a shortage. If the forge is shut down for any length of time the position might be more difficult, but probably some relief could be obtained by getting in forged parts from one of the other two factories making Rolls Royce engines.

The roof-spotters' warning was received two minutes before the bombs fell, but the men were rather slow in going to shelter and there were some casualties. However, the work people are unaffected by the raid and full night shifts were worked in all undamaged shops.

To summarise, the damage was caused in a particular shop which was not critical to production, and the intermediate stores of semi-finished parts will apparently be sufficient to prevent any loss of output. It will be a fortnight or so before this can be definitely confirmed. A full report will be prepared in due course by R.E. Department, Ministry of Home Security.

D.A.C. Dewdney,
S/Ldr.

31st July, 1942.

2

The initial official – top secret at the time – report of the bombing of the Rolls-Royce works at Nightingale Road in July 1942.

and I saw Derby straight before us. I knew exactly where to find my target and made straight for it. Suddenly we received a hit on the astrodome and felt a jar. A barrage balloon had touched us and been cut from its moorings.

"At the same moment we saw the works before us. The Oberste [*chief*] shouted: 'Out bombs, factory below us,' and I pressed the button and watched the bombs fall. There was a tremendous noise. The wind was blowing through the smashed astrodome and we couldn't hear much. We dived into the clouds as the plane had been badly damaged in the collision with the balloon. The right wing had been smashed.

"I turned for home under cover of clouds. These suddenly dispersed, and I saw an enemy fighter to our right. I nose-dived and reached another cloud. During the rest of the flight we were in high spirits at having succeeded."

The Dornier had flown over Rolls-Royce at 160ft, releasing four bombs, probably three 550kg and one 250kg. Only one hit the works itself, going through the roof of the Central Stores before entering the adjacent Steel Stores, where it exploded, wrecking both buildings as well as houses in Hawthorn Street, which backed on to the stores.

A second bomb scored a direct hit on Hawthorn Street, a third landed in gardens just a few yards away, and the fourth damaged houses in Abingdon Street and Handel Street. Altogether 23 people were killed either in the works or in neighbouring houses.

Former Sherwood Forester, Fred Day, was buried for seven hours. He recalled: "When the siren sounded, I went to the Central Stores to draw my rifle, as I was then in Royce's Home Guard, but the place was deserted except for a young girl sitting quite motionless at her typewriter. I begged her to go to the shelter but she just sat there. Then there was a loud bang and a hole appeared in the roof. I told her to tuck her head down with her hands behind it. Then there was a blinding flash, a huge explosion – and I woke up in hospital. They had dug me out around three in the afternoon. Later they told me that the young girl was killed when the bomb dropped. I suppose I was just lucky."

Edward Foulds remembered two girls with blackened faces running up and screaming: "Take cover, we've nearly been killed."

Tommy Broome was then the works manager: "Chaos reigned for a few minutes. There was dust, dirt and drizzle everywhere. I called for a runner to fetch 20 men and was told: 'What? It'll interfere with production.' Remarkably, we didn't lose a single engine, and by the third day production was back to normal. It was a remarkable effort."

Meanwhile, there was also chaos in the middle of Derby. Ron Till, who was then a 19-year-old mechanic employed by Babington Motors, remembered: "I stood rooted to the spot in utter amazement. A Dornier had snagged the balloon that flew overhead. He was so low I could see the black crosses under its wings, and the pilot, clear as day.

"Lady Luck was with that aircraft. When a balloon was hit, a cartridge-operated cable-shearing chisel arrangement was deployed which draped parachutes over the aircraft's wings. One of the parachutes caught on a lightning conductor on the Unity Hall opposite, and tore the parachute off. Otherwise the plane would have come down in the town centre." Over Chellaston, the Dornier that bombed Rolls-Royce had a similarly fortunate escape because the WAAF operating the balloon had not engaged the cartridge correctly and the balloon cable eventually slid off the aircraft's wing.

The "Babington Lane" Dornier made its escape, firing on a bus on Ashbourne Road as it flew north. The aircraft that had attacked Royce's escaped too, but in February 1943 it was shot down off Filey, while on a raid on Sunderland. It had a different crew by then, the four men who had bombed Derby having transferred to another Dornier, although they took part in the same raid.

Those who still claim that it was the same Dornier which bombed Royce's and strafed the centre of Derby, may like to consider the facts gathered by Messrs Kirk and Felix. There were three reported sightings of an aircraft at just before 8am that morning: to the south of Derby, at Weston-on-Trent, coming towards the town only 250ft above the railway line; to the south-west, over Burnaston; and to the north, at Duffield.

RAF records show there were two balloon impacts over Derby that day, one at Chellaston and one at Babington Lane. The pilot of the Dornier that bombed Rolls-Royce mentioned only one, on his way in from the south, obviously the Chellaston balloon. And why, after just having survived a perilous low-level bombing attack, would the aircraft which struck Rolls-Royce then hang around to indulge in some equally hazardous, and gratuitous, machine-gunning of traffic and pedestrians? Job done, it would surely have wanted to get high into the clouds and away from Derby's anti-aircraft barrage as soon as possible. That leaves just one myth to expel. The pilot of Dornier U5+LS had never worked at Rolls-Royce; in fact, not one of the four crew had ever set foot in the town.

The Best Christmas Present They Ever Had

"PUBLIC air-raid shelters have the reputation of being gloomy and depressing places, but when I went to the Abbey Street School shelter last night, I found a party and entertainment in full swing, the Searchlights Concert Party giving a show. The shelter was packed with a rollicking, happy audience." So the *Derby Evening Telegraph's* "Derby and Joan" column reported the mood in at least one part of Derby on Christmas Eve, 1940.

That second Christmas of the Second World War found the town trying hard to make the best of things. Derby had suffered its first casualties from German bombing, the sea war was going badly – Britain was a beleaguered island, her merchant shipping under constant threat from the U-boat menace – and the British Army still regrouping after the deliverance of the Dunkirk evacuation six months earlier.

It was going to be difficult to raise much Christmas spirit, but, back in Abbey Street, the party was in full swing, the shelter 'packed with a rollicking, happy audience'.

During the evening the caretaker, Mr J. Higgins, was presented with a watch and torch . He and the district's chief air-raid warden, Mr J. H. Doherty, had been among the first to realise that, with a little effort and imagination, air-raid shelters could be made more pleasant places.

The *Telegraph* reported: "Not only have they provided entertainments for the shelter user, encouraging them to look on the shelter as a centre of social activity, regardless of whether there is a raid in progress or not, they have also set to work on the shelter itself, providing poster decorations on the walls, rugs on the floor, and chairs."

On Christmas Day itself, the town was very quiet as people shut their front doors, closed the curtains and, if they were lucky enough to have the whole family at home, enjoyed themselves while they could.

Many family circles, though, were broken by the absence of husbands, sons and sweethearts serving in the forces. Knowing how they felt, many Derby families opened their homes to others spending Christmas away from their own people.

In Derby, factories, shops and offices were closed but hundreds of volunteers were on duty in the police, fire and civil defence services. Happily the town was almost free from accidents. The St Ambulance Brigade reported "the quietest Christmas on record" and the Derby Borough Police ambulance was called out only once, when John Gregory of Burton Road was in collision with a car near his home.

The Derby fire brigade were called out to only one incident, a chimney fire in Canal Street. None the less, the newspaper had to publish a health warning about the perils of stargazing during air-raids. Apparently one Derby man stood outside his house to admire the display made by bursting anti-aircraft shells, when a piece of shrapnel caught him a glancing blow on the head. "We can take it as official that he will know better henceforth," commented the *Evening Telegraph*.

There was one matter troubling "C.M", author of "A Derby Diary" in the *Evening Telegraph*. He asked: "Can Derby afford to give servicemen either free or cheaper-than-civic travel on its buses?" Apparently this had been done during the First World War. In the end, "C.M." came down in favour of the troops: "A concession of the sort would mean a lot to members of the forces who cannot always stay but in their own quarters."

On Christmas Eve 1941, "C.M." still appeared to be obsessed by bus stories: "Quite a number of people who do fire-watching in the centre of Derby live on the outskirts and depend on the Corporation bus service for transport. I hope those on the job will enjoy their walk home on Christmas morning. Meanwhile they will be interested to hear that Nottingham has decided to run certain special buses for the benefit of fire-watchers coming off duty at that time … Perhaps we can put it down to the fact that Nottinghamians are being pampered."

Meanwhile "The Sage", who penned the *Evening Telegraph's* "Candid Column", exhorted Derbeians to make the best of the war: "Do not mope this Christmas! You cannot win the war between now and Boxing Day, and you cannot help your absent relations and friends by refusing to accept the modest joys that the third wartime Christmas can offer you."

That could have meant, "Don't miss the pantomime." The Grand Theatre was staging *Babes in the Wood*. Consider this for a cast list: Tubby Turner, Lily Lapidus, Norman Langford, Hilary and Hazel Joyce, the 12 Famous Cholerton Juveniles, the 12 Drury Lane Babes, the Eileen Rogan Girls, and the Rapid Three, together with Blotto the Comedy Horse and a company of 50. "Give your kiddies a real Xmas treat" said the advertisement.

On Derby man unlikely to be enjoying his Christmas in 1941 was Frank Dolan of Stockbrook Street, who had just been sentenced to six months' imprisonment with hard labour after refusing to undergo a medical under National Service Act because he claimed to be a Jehovah's Witness.

Meanwhile, those Derby families with men serving in the Sherwood Foresters cast worried eyes over the war news. Earlier in the month, the Japanese had attacked Pearl Harbor and invaded Malaya. The 1st/5th Foresters had been diverted to Singapore. For most it would be their last Christmas of freedom for three years; indeed, many would never see another Christmas at all.

By December 1942, however, the war on other fronts had turned the Allies' way following victory in North Africa. For some there was now a reason to celebrate, and on Christmas Eve, the *Evening Telegraph* reported that Christmas trees were growing in the Western Desert: "The advance of the Eighth Army seems well-timed to coincide with Christmas because in the area 40 miles to the east of Benghazi grow probably the only Christmas trees in North Africa."

The newspaper concluded that the shimmering sands and consuming heat must have been an unusual backdrop for the singing of Irving Berlin's *I'm Dreaming of a White Christmas*.

It was also reported that Derby Cathedral and other churches would ring their bells on Christmas morning, and there would be special Christmas morning treats for some local children.

Seventy-five Derby boys and girls aged 12 and under, whose fathers were prisoners-of-war, would receive presents from American schoolchildren in Brooklyn and White Plains, in New York state, and New Jersey respectively.

One lucky three-year-old would receive red, white and blue mittens, a book, a rubber ball, a motor-car, crayons, pencils and a tablet of soap.

In Derby's open market on Christmas Eve 1942, apples were almost unobtainable, grapes available at an astonishing 24s (£1.20) per pound. At one stall there was a long queue for tomatoes, but fresh vegetables were freely available. There was also an orange scam.

One Derby fruiterer told the *Evening Telegraph* that when a new supply of oranges had arrived, in accordance with Ministry of Food regulations he had sold them to children under 18 for the first five days. But women from Belper had arrived with children's ration books and he had been forced to sell to them. It appeared that Belper's fruiterers were selling oranges to anybody who had the money. So locals had been forced to come to Derby, and now Derby's children were missing out.

By Christmas 1943, the war, although far from won, had turned again in the Allies' favour. Italy had been invaded by the British and Americans, and in the Far East, the Japanese had been driven out of the Gilbert Islands. Thousands of Derby men, and some women, were now serving all over the globe and letters from home were precious. So, too, were communications from service personnel to their loved ones left behind. The *Evening Telegraph* reported that it had been "teamwork" which had made possible the complete delivery of Derby's Christmas mail. Post Office regulars, together with temporary staff, had ensured the mail got through despite a bout of influenza at the LMS Station which had laid low so many porters that administrative staff had to be brought in to handle parcel traffic.

On Christmas Day 1943, the Mayor of Derby, Alderman E. A. Armstrong, did the usual rounds of hospitals and workhouses. Unusually, he also visited Derby Synagogue on Burton Road, where he met members of the town's Hebrew congregation, as well as 100 Jewish members of the armed forces stationed locally. They were mostly British and Americans but included one Pole and one Czech, and several members of the ATS.

Finally, there was the happy story of brothers Albert and Alf Handley of Stockbrook Street. Trooper Albert Handley, who had been wounded twice, was in the company office of the Derbyshire Yeomanry in Algeria when a dispatch rider entered. It was brother, Alf, who, discovering where Albert was stationed, jumped on his motor-cycle and drove 600 miles to deliver a dispatch in the area in the hope that they might meet up. They had not seen each other for two years, and both agreed – it was the best Christmas present they had ever had.

Sergeant Theresa Wallach (standing) was already a famous woman motorcyclist and adventurer when she arrived in Derby in August 1941 to head an ATS recruiting campaign. Wallach served in the Army Transport Corps, first as a mechanic and later as the first woman motorcycle dispatch rider in the British Army.

Wartime provided new work opportunities for women. These two are learning the secrets of the Derby Corporation bus that they will soon be driving in March 1943. Notes the vehicle's hooded headlights.

Local Army cadets line up for their breakfast at Chatsworth in August 1942.

Under the nose of a bomber, wartime Derby members of the Air Training Corps receive instructions.

Air Training Corps recruits sign on at Alvaston in February 1941.

An instructor shows pupil pilots how to swing a propeller at RAF Burnaston in March 1941.

These members of an RAF barrage balloon section were stationed on Alvaston Park in 1941.

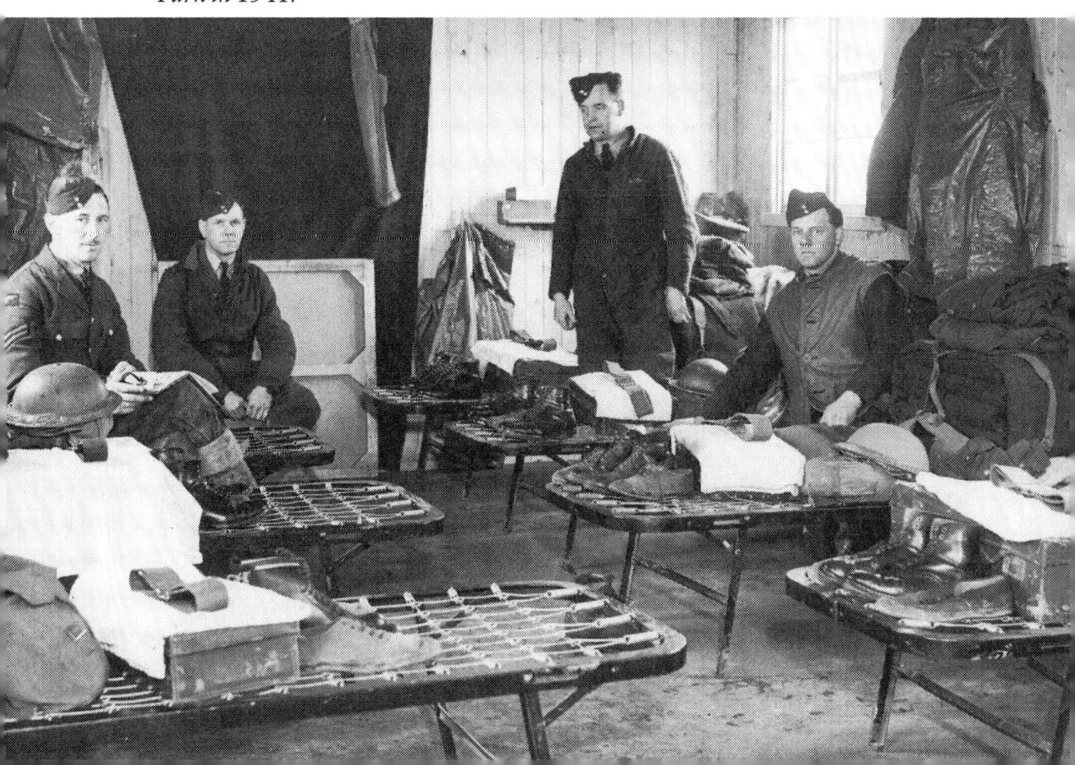

Over-sexed and Over Here

A DERBY soldier, home on leave and walking down Green Lane in September 1942, snapped a salute at two men in resplendent military uniform, and was astonished when they collapsed with laughter. The reason for their amusement was simple enough: far from being high-ranking officers, they were simple "doughboys" – GIs – from the United States Army which had taken up quarters at Weston-on-Trent the previous day.

The humble private from Derby wouldn't make the same mistake again, and the US uniform would soon become a familiar sight in the town. Soon, with the help of local labour, the Americans had built one of the biggest US bases in the country, on land between Egginton and Sudbury. It held over 8,000 GIs and contained miles of road and railway sidings. From that moment there was an influx of many thousands of American troops into the Derby area. The Red Cross opened special clubs for them, while pubs in Derby began to sound more like the bars of cattle country in the American West.

There was also a strict colour bar in operation. White and black troops were allowed into Derby on different nights and the white helmeted, white-gaitered US military police patrolled the streets, calling into pubs to ensure that the US's own segregation laws were not broken. Black troops might be good enough to die alongside their white colleagues; drinking with them was an entirely different matter.

Generally, though, local people disliked the colour bar, and, black or white, American soldiers were certainly a source of wonderment to many local women. For a start they had more money – "overpaid, oversexed and over here" was the complaint from local men – and they also represented a glamorous world which hitherto had been viewed only through the Hollywood movies shown nightly at Derby's many cinemas.

Of course, most GIs were not the product of Hollywood, but that did not prevent local women from imagining that they were. Who was the better companion – the boyfriend who toiled long hours at the Carriage and Wagon Works and had little, if any, money to spend on nights out? Or the seemingly sophisticated American in the smart uniform, the man with the western drawl and a wallet full of notes?

Efforts had been made on both sides to alleviate resentment. The BBC broadcast a series of radio talks entitled *Let's Get Acquainted*, and the US Army produced a leaflet *Over There: Instructions for American Servicemen in Britain, 1942*. The latter reminded troops: "You are higher paid than the British Tommy. Don't rub it in. Play fair with him. He could be a pal in need."

American troops stationed on the outskirts of Derby were also reminded not to boast that America had won the last war. And they were implicitly warned: "Don't play into Hitler's hands by mentioning war debts."

In August 1997, Elsie Church told her grandson, Peter King: "In Derby when the Americans came, the black Americans came and the white Americans came. In Derby they had separate nights for them both to be out. They never let both the black and the white Americans in town together, because there was still a bit of tension. They were lovely boys the black boys were. You had nothing to be afraid of. They were good lads."

Favourite haunts for the Americans in Derby were the pubs in Sadler Gate and the Market Place – the Half Moon, the Bell, the Shakespeare, the Globe and the Wine Vaults. The Americans were not always welcome visitors, however.

Those stationed at Eggington Hall left several upstairs taps running when they left for the good. The resultant flooding added to the house's general decay and it was eventually considered beyond repair and demolished.

December 1941 and the Japanese attack on Pearl Harbor had seen the US enter the war, and if the following year brought many of their troops to Derby, 1942 was also a year when the people of the town had finally got to grips with life in wartime Britain.

They had survived the immediate threat of invasion and the prospect of German paratroopers descending from the sky. They had also survived the worst of the bombing. From now on, the air-raid sirens would be less frequent, nights in the shelter slowly abandoned for a return to the warmth of a comfortable bed. And they had adapted to – if not accepted – the restrictions and inconveniences that the war had inevitably brought to their doorsteps. Indeed, for many, looking back years later, it was almost a happy time.

Alex McWilliams was working at Rolls-Royce in 1942 and he recalled: "Without doubt there was something indefinable about life in Derby at the time. We'd weathered the very worst that the Germans could throw at us, and now things were beginning to level out a bit. We couldn't actually see any light at the end of a very long tunnel, but at least we had begun to feel our way around in the gloom.

"I suppose it was because we all had something to fight for, and we had a common enemy. Men and women got up and went to work for long shifts, went home to snatch some sleep, and then back to work, or perhaps on to Home Guard duty. They didn't grumble. There was a job to be done and they just got on with it.

"It was an attitude which spilled over into everything we did, even sport. When we played football or cricket, we played it hard but we played it fair. People knew that, ultimately, we were all on the same side."

Derby was certainly busy working for the war effort in 1942. Warships Week opened on February 28, and raised £1,941,657 to pay for the cruiser HMS *Kenya*, which was adopted by the town. Wings for Victory raised £1,668,358 in the town.

In 1943, the upward trend in Derby's wartime fortunes continued. The first Derby men to be repatriated from German PoW camps arrived home. Some of them had been missing since they were left behind with the remnants of the BEF at Dunkirk.

From abroad came news of Allied successes in North Africa, in particular the epic deeds of the Derbyshire Yeomanry. As Winston Churchill told the nation, if it wasn't exactly the beginning of the end, then it was at least the end of the beginning.

By the autumn of 1943, a record 130,000-acre harvest waited to be gathered in Derbyshire, and hundreds of factory workers and children gave up their summer holidays to work in the fields alongside Italian prisoners of war.

There was also a major upheaval in the social order. A shortage of labour was responsible for the complete disappearance of postmen from the streets of Derby as deliveries were maintained exclusively by women. Women bus drivers, an unthinkable sight before the war, also appeared.

The reasons were simple enough: those men who were not working in vital reserved occupations were away in the services, at sea, on land and in the air. Derby was doing its bit in every theatre of the war. Just as the Americans were over here, thousands of Derbeians were over there.

In Every Major Battle ...

'THROUGHOUT the war, few military units have played such a notable part as Derbyshire's own regiments, the Sherwood Foresters and the Derbyshire Yeomanry. In every major battle one or the other – sometimes both – have been in the thick of the fray." So said the *Derby Evening Telegraph* in May 1945.

Yet the fortunes of war gave the two regiments vastly differing roles. While the Yeomanry enjoyed spectacular moments of triumph, the Foresters had a grimmer tale to tell. Their part had been played in some of the more tragic episodes of the war.

The Foresters were the first to go into action. Three battalions were in France when Germany invaded Belgium in May 1940. They were in the vanguard of the British Expeditionary Force which advanced to Brussels. Doggedly though they fought to stem the German advance, the Foresters suffered severe casualties. Derby men with the 5th Battalion fought with Ark Force, formed to support the 51st Highland Division in their lone, desperate action near St Valery. But only a fraction of them fought their way through Fecamp to Le Harve. Among those taken prisoner was the CO, Lt-Col H. B. Everard.

The 8th Battalion of the Foresters served with the British force in Norway, but the next major battle involving the regiment was in the Western Desert. A battalion faced Rommel's drive from the Gazala line in May 1942. As Rommel swept towards Egypt, the Foresters retreated into Tobruk and went down in the inexplicable collapse of the crucial bastion. Their losses were so heavy that by June the battalion ceased to exist as a separate unit.

The Tobruk debacle of 1942 – Winston Churchill called the whole affair "a disgrace" with 35,000 British troops and a priceless array of military equipment captured – was the Foresters' third major disaster of the war. In February that year, the 1st/5th Battalions, reformed after their losses in France, had sailed from Liverpool in late October 1941, aboard the converted P&O liner, the troopship *Orchids*, for an unknown destination.

The 1st/5th Foresters, along with the 1st Battalion the Cambridgeshire Regiment, and the 5th Battalion Bedfordshire and Hertfordshire Regiment, formed one of the three brigades of the British 18th Division, 55 Brigade. They were destined for the Middle East but were diverted to Singapore after the Japanese invasion of Malaya in December 1941. The Foresters arrived just before the Japanese made their final assault across the causeway that linked Malaya with Singapore. The Derby men were too late to influence the course of a bitter and confused battle, and almost to a man they were captured, although a handful escaped and eventually made their way to India.

It was 18 months before the first printed PoW cards arrived in Derby. The cards bore stereotyped messages and the only handwriting was the men's signatures. Nevertheless, they did much to relieve the intense anxiety of their loved ones. Those Foresters who fell into Japanese hands worked like slaves on road construction and many were interned in Siam (modern Thailand).

There were many tales of heroism and one liberated PoW told the *Derby Evening Telegraph* of the stand made by Lt-Col Harold

Lilly, the Foresters' CO, during a forced march in which the prisoners had to cover 85 miles to Wampo – where they were put to work on the infamous Burma Railway – in less than six days.

"Our boys were dropping dead from exhaustion and Lt-Col Lilly said: 'My men are just too exhausted to march.' The Japanese officer said: 'Do you know I can have you shot for refusing to march?'

"Our CO replied: 'You'd better shoot me then, because we are not marching.' And we didn't march."

Harold Lilly was born in Spondon in 1888 and had seen action on the Somme during the First World War. After the fall of Singapore, he had charge of 1,500 prisoners of war, almost one third of whom would die in the mosquito-infested jungle, in searing heat and almost unbearable humidity. Lilly died only nine years after the Foresters' liberation, his men still talking with emotion of his relentless efforts to protect those in his charge, often taking beatings on their behalf.

Meanwhile, despite the change in fortunes heralded by the successful North African campaign, there was yet more suffering for the Foresters in another theatre of the war. In Tunisia, a company of the 2nd/5th Battalion, surrounded by the enemy, stood and fought to the last man.

After the invasion of Italy, the Foresters won notable successes, but again they needed all their indomitable spirit and courage. Just behind the beaches at Salerno, they faced the Germans for five days without yielding an inch of ground.

On the Volturno, attacked from the rear, the Foresters lost their CO, second-in-command, padre and MO in fighting their way out of the trap. Anzio saw the Foresters again in the thick of the battle and two officers each won the Military Cross. Even when the war had ended, the regiment's ordeal was not over. Sherwood Foresters were among the 144 British and Australian prisoners rescued from a Japanese transport sunk in the Pacific in September 1945. They gave the first accounts of their lives under the Japanese when, despite every difficulty, they arranged sporting and cultural activities. They had even managed to hold a thanksgiving service when news filtered through of the Allied invasion of Normandy in June 1944.

IT was as desert fighters that the Derbyshire Yeomanry first achieved distinction during the Second World War. In the words of one military observer: "They were legendary for their daring and extreme efficiency. Wherever there was a battle, they were always first in. And, if a withdrawal was to be carried out, they were the last to leave."

An armoured car unit of the Derbyshire Yeomanry left Britain in April 1942 and fought with the Eighth Army from the following August. Another unit arrived in North Africa with the First Army in November 1942 and eventually gained world fame as the first Allied troops to enter Tunis. In the whole of that campaign they took 10,000 prisoners at a cost of only 107 casualties.

May 7, 1943, was the historic day that Lt Peter Adeley led the troopers of C squadron along the main Massicault-Tunis road at the height of the battle for North Africa.

After linking up with a troop of 11th Hussars, the Yeomanry patrol moved swiftly into the city and took the Germans by surprise, Many surrendered without a struggle.

Minutes later, Adeley radioed the message for which the world had been waiting: "Tunis entered." Before long, tanks from the 7th Armoured Division were pouring into the city.

Although there is some debate about the Yeomanry's claim – some say that it should at least be shared with the 11th Hussars – military historians generally accept that it is Derbyshire's honour. Certainly, when the Deputy Prime Minister, Clement Attlee, announced the fall of Tunis to the House of Commons, he gave the credit to the Derbyshire regiment.

Less than a week after the capture of Tunis, Captain John Davie of the Derbyshire Yeomanry sat in a small orchard just inland from Bou Ficha. It was 13 May and the battle for Tunisia had all but been won.

Suddenly a voice crackled in his headphones: "Hello, British Eight Army. This the Italian First Army."

Captain Davie replied: "This is the British First Army. You cannot speak to the Eighth Army, so you had better speak to me. Is it that you wish to surrender?"

After some hesitation, during which Captain Davie told the Italians that they were the last Axis troops holding out in North Africa, the Italians said they would surrender only if accorded the full honours of war.

As this would mean a surrender with fixed bayonets, drums beating and colours flying, Captain Davie refused and that evening the Italian commander drove to Bou Ficha in person, waving a white flag.

In Italy, the Yeomanry were equipped with tanks for the first time when they figured in the great battle for the Gustav Line. Again the regiment wrote its name into the history of the Second World War, this time with a "do-or-die" charge by its commanding officer.

On 14 May, 1944, after the squadron leader had been killed by a sniper's bullet, Colonel Peter Payne-Galway leapt into his tank and led the squadron into action with a tommy gun in one hand and a grenade in the other.

An officer takes up the story: " The colonel was standing in the turret like a man possessed, firing his tommy gun...Only when he had knocked out the gun holding us up , did he return to his command post."

In five days the Derbyshire Yeomanry advanced eight miles through a line which the Germans had boasted was impregnable. As one German prisoner put it: "It's no use, your guns fire everywhere."

The Derbyshire Yeomanry were also in evidence in Normandy when they helped to hold the Orne bridgehead, and later led their division over the Seine and into Belgium, Holland and Germany – a feat which earned them the nickname of the "Mad Recce".

Derby husbands, sons, brothers and sweethearts distinguished themselves in every corner of the world, not only in the Foresters and the Yeomanry but also in countless other regiments, in the air and on the sea, as they fought for Derby at war.

War Reserve police trainees pictured at Derby in 1945.

In March 1941, troops from a cavalry remount depot utilise their spare time to plough land adjacent to Derby Racecourse that has been given over the arable use.

ATS members ready themselves to set off in convoy from Derby during the fierce winter of 1940-41.

After reporting to Normanton Barracks in 1940, these recruits relax around a game of snooker.

War in the Air

WHEN Derby Airport was officially opened in the summer of 1939, there were still precious few local people who could ever have dreamt of taking a holiday by air. Flying off to France or Jersey was the preserve of the very well-to-do. Most Derbeians did not even own a car. Holidays meant climbing abroad a train at the LMS station, or Friargate, or catching a Trent bus to the seaside.

Yet, for quite a number local men, the experience of air travel was just around the corner. It would, though, hardly be a relaxing experience. Many would soon find themselves learning to fly with the Royal Air Force. That summer, as war clouds gathered over Europe, the British Government began, belatedly, to address the issue of aerial warfare, and the Derby area would soon see a rapid expansion of military airfields. Air Force blue would be a familiar sight in the town's pubs and shops. Eventually, American, Australian, Czech and Polish fliers would join British airmen wandering through Derby's streets on a rare day off.

The "Brylcreem Boys" had arrived in the neighbourhood.

It came as no real surprise, however. By the time it was officially opened as Derby's municipal airport in June 1939, Burnaston aerodrome was already a military base, housing the RAF Volunteer Reserve Training Centre, formed a year earlier.

No. 30 Elementary and Reserve Training School, RAF, had been formed on 29 September 1938, run by Air Schools Ltd under Captain N. Roy Harben DFC, who had also formed Derby Aero Club.

After the outbreak of war, No. 27 E & RFTS arrived and amalgamated to form No 30 Elementary Flying Training School. The unit was equipped with Tiger Moths, Miles Magisters, Hawker Harts and Fairey Battles and soon the little yellow training aircraft became a familiar sight in the skies over Derby.

A former *Derby Evening Telegraph* editor, Bob Randall, remembered when "a kink in the training programme at Burnaston gave me months of pleasant flying in Tiger Moths, one of the benefits of which was seeing the town of Derby in context".

At the height of the invasion scare in 1940, the aircraft were fitted with bomb racks and, in the same year, a stick of German incendiaries fell on the Burnaston airfield but no aircraft were damaged.

Under wartime conditions, Burnaston expanded rapidly and soon had four grass runways, but, even then, the aerodrome could not cope with the demand placed upon it. Satellite airfields were provided at Battlestead Hill, near Tatenhill, and Abbots Bromley, near Uttoxeter. For a time, the US 8th Army Air Corps shared Abbots Bromley with the RAF

Throughout the war, training was Burnaston's main role and the original development of the Link Trainer – to become a standard part of any pilot's training – was carried out here when the airfield employed around 300 local civilians as well as military personnel.

Besides trainee bomber pilots, army corporals were taught to fly gliders as part of the fledgling Glider Pilot Regiment. They came to Burnaston to take a 12-week course to qualify as light aircraft pilots before being sent on to Glider Training School. Although Burnaston resumed its role as Derby Airport after the war, the RAF did not close their No. 3 Basic Flying School there until 21 July 1953.

Further down the A38, work began on RAF Lichfield, known locally as Fradley. One of Fradley's satellite airfields was RAF Church Broughton, about ten miles from Derby. For some time, Church Broughton was the home of No 1429 (Czech) Operational Training Flight, which flew Wellingtons.

In his book *The Day The Dump Went Up & The Flying Kangaroos* journalist Mark Rowe recounts the story of Jaroslav Havlik, from Prague, who trained as a pilot for pleasure before the war. During his stay at Church Broughton, Jaroslav had to enter Derby City Hospital for a cartilage operation. There he met Vera, a 24-year-old nurse, and fell in love. Wartime romance was never easy. Vera and Jaroslav had their separate duties, and transport was scarce. Vera said: "I never went to Church Broughton because he had a cycle and I used to leave it to him to come to Derby."

In 1943, Jaroslav was posted to South Wales, where he survived his aircraft crashing on take-off. The couple married and settled in

Britain, Jaroslav working as a photographer for the National Coal Board at Bretby. The Havliks had two sons and two daughters. Jaroslav Havlik died in 1975.

On Sunday afternoons, people came from Derby and lined the road to watch the aircraft taking off and landing at Church Broughton as Australian pilots out on something of a flying show. Indeed, Australian airmen based there were a familiar sight in Derby's pubs. Mark Rowe tells of a February 1944 entry in the diary of Flying Officer Brian Cosgriff, a trainee bomb aimer, who enjoyed a blind date in Derby: "A very nice and decent girl. We had a few drinks and then went to the Plaza to dance – very good."

Gwen Smith told Mr Rowe that, as Gwen Canlin, a teenage WAAF from Ilkeston, who from 1943 to 1945 served as a driver at Church Broughton, she saw the Australians experience their first snowfall. "They were snowballing us and rubbing our faces in it," she said.

Like most RAF stations, Church Broughton saw its share of tragedy, and the graves of airmen at Scropton Church are proof enough. One incident stands out: on the evening of 14 January, 1945, Flying Officer Kevin Cranley and his fellow Australians took off in their Wellington for a flight over the North Sea. The aircraft was attacked by a German night fighter and on its return, Canley found most of the UK fogbound.

Just before midnight, he attempted an emergency landing at Wymeswold, a few miles east of Loughborough, but the bomber crashed close to the airfield and caught fire. Canley, the pilot, and Jack Hann, the bomb aimer, both unconscious in the burning plane, were rescued by the wireless operator, Jim Reuter, but Eric Peace, an air gunner, was killed. The remainder of the crew recovered from their injuries and all survived the war.

American airmen were also a familiar sight. During the latter part of 1943, the 337th Service Squadron left New York harbour aboard the *SS Slauterdyke* bound for Britain. After a very rough crossing of the north Atlantic, their ship docked at Glasgow. The squadron then boarded a train that took them to a holding base near Long Eaton. Before being assigned to the 437th TCG in Wiltshire during the early weeks of 1944, the US airmen had plenty of time to hop on a bus and sample the delights of Derby's pubs.

Work on RAF Ashbourne began in 1941, when a farm and several private houses fringing Derby Road were demolished. Ashbourne aerodrome opened in the summer of 1942, as a training airfield in 38 Group.

In July that year, No 81 Operational Training Unit was established at Ashbourne, flying Wellingtons. In October, No 42 OTU arrived and was divided into four separate units, training on Blenheims, Whitleys and Albermarles.

From June 1943 to February 1945, Darley Moor, south of Ashbourne, was used as a satellite airfield, where air gunners and wireless operators were trained on Ansons and Oxfords.

In March 1945, the unit was disbanded and Ashbourne closed to flying. No 28 Maintenance Unit moved in and the runways were used to store bombs until they could be moved to the Derbyshire moors and destroyed.

Ashbourne aerodrome finally closed in 1954. Today it is the site of a light industrial park. Darley Moor, meanwhile, became a home for motorcycle racing.

RAF Castle Donington was opened on New Year's Day, 1943, 18 months after the area was first surveyed as part of Air Ministry plans to build a number of new bomber stations for the Midlands.

It became a satellite for RAF Wymeswold as part of 92 Group. Castle Donington was used by part of 28 OTU, equipped with Wellingtons. Later, Martinets and Masters were used for target towing, later still to be replaced by Hurricanes. July 1943 saw the start of a short-lived scheme to train crews of the Pathfinder Force.

After D-Day, Castle Donington was transferred to Transport Command, equipped with 40 Dakota aircraft. The station became a vital link in the setting up of trunk routes to liberated countries and the ferrying of troops and supplies along these routes.

Castle Donington was abandoned by the RAF in 1946, but when it became clear that Derby's civil airport at Burnaston could not be developed to meet growing post-war needs, Castle Donington was selected to replace it.

Thus, on 1 April 1965, East Midlands Airport opened. Gone were the Wellingtons, Hurricanes, Stirlings and Yorks. A new breed of aircraft now transported a new breed of passenger.

No account of the local connection with the wartime RAF would be complete without mentioning 617 Squadron. In 1943, the Dambusters trained over the Derwent and Howden dams, practising the low-level flying techniques which would help them deliver Ripley-born Barnes Wallis's "bouncing bomb" to Germany's industrial heartland.

By the end of that year, the tide of war was turning in the Allies' favour. Along with the rest of the free world, Derby waited anxiously for that great moment when victory came within reach.

Great Events Impending

BY the end of 1943, Derby folks felt that victory could soon be within the Allies' grasp as the tide of war had turned in their favour.

The end of the North African campaign, in which the Derbyshire Yeomanry had figured so spectacularly, and the sweep from the beaches of Salerno and Anzio into Italy, had left the Allies with the opportunity and the resources to stage the operation for which everyone was waiting – the invasion of France.

By the spring of 1944, the people of Derby knew that an Allied invasion of the European mainland could not be far off. Personnel of the National Fire Service, barrage balloons and heavy anti-aircraft batteries left the town to defend the Channel ports, where there was a massive build-up of Allied troops. The defence of Derby was left with the local Home Guard units and their "Z" rocket batteries.

Road and rail traffic southwards increased and the canvas covers could not disguise the tell-tale shapes of landing craft. Column after column of tanks and armoured cars snaked their way around the edge of the town, heading south, and overhead Dakotas towed gliders through the skies. The military camps around Derby became deserted as the huge invasion army was assembled on the south coast.

One night in April, Derbeians thought that the invasion had begun when a huge air convoy created an impressive spectacle as the green and red navigation lights of both gliders and transport planes made a brilliant pattern in Derby's night sky. That was a false dawn, but as invasion day grew ever nearer, the significance of this truly awesome adventure came home fully to the men and women working long shifts to produce munitions in Derby's factories, or simply gossiping in the pub – when beer was available – or the corner shop.

If it succeeded, then surely it would herald the end of all the pain and suffering, and the paraphernalia of war would at last be removed from Derby's streets. But what if it failed? Apart from the obvious military disaster, people began to wonder if they would have the energy to begin all over again, exhausted as they were by a war which was originally going to be "over by Christmas" but which had already lasted five years.

As June 1944 came, the people of Derby went to bed each night with a sense of great events impending. They knew that any day now would come the news of the battle that would alter the course of their lives, and the lives of their children, for ever.

On the morning of 6 June 1944, the newspapers and early morning radio news were full of the fall of Rome, which had been announced the day before. But just after 9am, came the brief announcement: "Under the command of General Eisenhower, Allied naval forces supported by strong air forces began landing Allied armies this morning on the coast of France."

The battle was joined and one Derby man in the thick of it was 20-year-old Gerald Mumby from Twyford Street, who had been working at the Inland Revenue Office in Gower Street before being called-up to join the Royal Navy. In June 1943, along with young David Brindley, of the well-known ladies' clothing shop in Babington Lane, he reported to HMS Royal Arthur, a shore base at Butlin's, Skegness. It was the beginning of a great adventure because he was one of the first ashore on D-Day.

"I was serving as a naval telegraphist. I landed at 8.30am, on Gold Beach with a forward observation bombardment unit. There were three of us in an armoured 9-ton half-track: me, an artillery officer, and an artillery bombardier, who was the driver.

"The officer would work out where he wanted our ships offshore to aim their shells, then I would relay the bearings to the ships.

"I was lucky because our bit of the beach was relatively quiet; there were only a few bodies about. But of the 100 FOB units that went ashore, only 30 returned.

"As we were preparing to drive ashore off the landing craft, the jeep in front went straight down into the sea and sank. Then we couldn't get through because the sand dunes had been mined and we had to wait for them to be cleared. We were on the beach until about 11am, then we could move inland.

"About 20 years ago, I went back with my wife and son and retraced the route where we went in. I even found the spot where I'd dug a slit trench."

After his role in D-Day, Gerald Mumby returned to the UK but eventually found himself en route to the Far East. He was off the coast of Malaya when the Allies dropped atomic bombs on Hiroshima and Nagasaki and the war ended. Then he landed at Singapore and later worked his way through the Philippines, helping to liberate prison camps.

But that was all in the future. Hardly had the Normandy beachheads been established when Derby began to see something of the other side of the picture. On 13 June, only a week after D-Day, the first convoy of wounded soldiers arrived at the LMS Station. A grim procession of stretchers carried casualties from trains to the waiting ambulances. Men in hospital blue became a familiar sight in Derby.

Before long, the effects of the Germans' campaign of "flying-bombs" – the V1s and later V2s that terrorised southern cities – began to be felt. Even though Derby did not see first-hand these latest weapons of mass destruction, the first 'doodlebug' evacuees began to arrive, first in a trickle and then in a flood as the official scheme were made fully operative. Between July and September, when the Allies captured the rocket sites in northern Holland, Derby received 8,000 evacuees.

Meanwhile, the Allied advances in Italy had freed many Derby prisoners-of-war. Most had escaped by the time of the Italian capitulation and played hide and seek with German and Italian fascist groups for almost a year before it was safe to emerge into the arms of the advancing victorious armies. In early August 1944, a group of former PoWs arrived in Derby with tales of their precarious existence in the Italian countryside as they dodged the retreating army.

With Allied armies now firmly established in Occupied Europe, the last thing that the people of Derby were thinking about was danger from the air. Yet on 31 August 1944, that is exactly what happened. The aircraft were a Tiger Moth and an Airspeed Oxford, which collided before the Moth fell with a terrific crash and a huge sheet of flame. Among schoolchildren on their way to lessons at the time was Barry Helliwell, then a seven-year-old schoolboy living in South Avenue, Chellaston. He remembers the crash well.

"Another couple of minutes and we would all probably have been killed. It was awful. The Tiger Moth came down on Derby Road with the pilot trapped inside. It was a fireball and people just knelt on the road and wept and prayed. There was nothing anybody could do."

Overhead the pilot of the Airspeed Oxford, which had half its wing torn off, managed to steer the machine clear of the village in a heroic and selfless attempt to save lives. Just before his plane crashed in a field off Sinfin Moor Lane the pilot bailed out, but he was far too low to save his own life.

It was a reminder that the war was far from over, but when, in March 1945, the first consignment of lemons to be seen in the town for three years arrived in Derby, it was one of those small but significant events which signalled that a return to pre-war normality might not be far away.

December 1944 saw the Home Guard lay down their arms. They had never been called into action, but they would have been ready to defend the town against German invaders had the call come. Two days before Christmas, Derby Corporation bus crews went on strike in a dispute over new timetables. Rumours of the action had spread and most shoppers had gone home at lunchtime, thus avoiding the disruption.

The war news, meanwhile, was hardly cheering. In the Ardennes, Field Marshall Gerd von Rundstedt was making a desperate attempt to break through Allied lines, although on Christmas Day itself, the US 2nd Armoured Division stopped the 2nd Panzer Division reaching the River Meuse. Nevertheless, the German counter-offensive had been a setback, and after all all the euphoria of D-Day and its aftermath, the British people were again beginning to wonder, just when would it all end? The war that was going to over by Christmas, back in 1939, had a little way to run yet.

Victory

THE *Evening Telegraph* newspaper seller hurrying through Derby Bus Station was doing a passable imitation of the Pied Piper of Hamelin. Hundreds of people flocked after him and within two minutes of receiving his latest supply of papers, he had sold out.

Seventy years later, many of those newspapers survive, souvenirs of one of the most momentous days in British history – Tuesday, 8 May 1945, VE Day – their headline signalling the end of the war in Europe.

After six long war-weary years, 148 air-raid alerts, 152 high-explosive bombs, 164 incendiary bombs, 45 civilian deaths due to enemy action, and between 3,000 and 4,000 houses damaged, the end was near.

In early May 1945, people knew it could be only a matter of time before peace was announced, and they gathered around their wireless sets all over Derby. The first news that the end had come was heard, ironically, through German radio.

Everyone knew that the German surrender was imminent and by mid-morning there were already 2,000 people in Derby Market

Place before a violent midday thunderstorm sent them scurrying for cover. The Bishop of Derby reminded them: "We have won a victory over Germany. Be satisfied with that. Don't grumble about the weather."

By 2pm, the sun was shining again and the victory celebrations went into full swing. Trolley bus standards were swathed in bunting, and loudspeakers replayed speeches by the King and Winston Churchill, the Prime Minister. Others joined amateur musicians with saxophones, accordions, dustbin lids, tin cans and anything else that would make a noise. One US military policeman was surrounded and had all his equipment removed while a saloon car was pushed around the square before being ripped to pieces. The crowd's repertoire seemed to consist of just three songs: *There'll Always Be An England*; *Pack Up Your Troubles*; and *Roll Out The Barrel*.

At the Plaza Ballroom, police were called to eject hundreds of gatecrashers to Sam Ramsden's private party at which George Elrick, later to win fame on television's *New Faces* talent-spotting programme in the 1970s, was playing with his band.

Street parties lasted all week. In Stockbrook Street blackout material was burned to the solemn accompaniment of a gramophone wheezing out *There'll Always Be An England*, and in Agard Street, on the edge of Derby's West End, a piano was wheeled into the street.

On Osmaston Road, a shopkeeper had effigies of Hitler and Goreing hanging from his premises, while in Brook Street another Hitler dummy bore the sentiment: "Adolf, you've had it."

By midnight on 8 May 1945, it was impossible to estimate the number of people who had thronged the Market Place. In Green Lane, the Beaconsfield Club had to enlist the help of the NFS turntable ladder to raise the Union Flag on the building's flagpole. The other option, climbing out on to the roof via an attic window, was declared to dangerous.

The violent midday storm broke up a British Legion parade following a service at St Werburgh's Church. It erupted as the parade passed the Mayor and Mayoress of Derby, Councillor and Mrs W. H. Phillips, and Lt-Col C. C. Stepney, who were taking the salute in the Market Place.

August 1945 and crowds in Derby Market Place celebrate the end of the war in the Far East.

The wind whipped off hats and the downpour soaked hundreds of people. The participants held fast until they had passed the saluting base, and then dived for cover. The British Legion Band stopped half way through the march and dashed into a shop doorway until the worst of the storm had abated.

The residents of Norman Street in New Normanton collected £90 for their party and everywhere carefully stored-up rations were at last unwrapped as the parties began. Both the Midland Station and the Cavendish were also decorated with bunting and flags.

The first weather forecast since the outbreak of war had been published on 4 May and had predicted "sporadic outbreaks of rain and the possibility of thunder". The peak temperature was reached on 9 May when the mercury rose to nearly 72 degree Fahrenheit.

By then Darley Park looked more like Blackpool beach at the start of the season; there was a three and a half hour wait for rowing boats on Alvaston Lake; at the Arboretum, 7,000 happy people watched the Searchlights Concert Party; and 3,000 flocked to Normanton Park to hear the Derby Borough Military Band.

There was football, too. Peter Doherty scored both goals for Derby County when they drew 2-2 with neighbours Nottingham Forest in a victory match.

A crowd of almost 7,000 saw the game at the bomb-damaged Baseball Ground, among them the coal merchant from Horsley Woodhouse who, later that month, was find £1 10s £1.50) by Derby magistrates for "misuse of petrol". His crime? He had driven his son to the Baseball Ground to watch the Rams.

The magistrates were not attempting sarcasm; it was simply that in the days when posters asked: 'Is Your Journey Really Necessary?' watching football as hardly considered essential.

For those who wanted to get indoors on that hot, humid week, there was a choice of 16 cinemas in Derby, showing films ranging from Joan Fontaine in *Frenchman's Creek* , adapted from the Daphne du Maurier novel, at the Hippodrome (the theatre in Green Lane then enjoying a new career as a cinema) to James Cagney and Humphrey Bogart in *The Roaring Twenties* at the Cosmo in Upper Boundary Road.

There was also one theatre, the Grand in Babington Lane, where the Ballets Jooss company held their own quiet celebration backstage after their production had finished for the evening. Before the show the national anthems of Britain, France, the United States and the Soviet Union were played.

Yet in the midst of all this euphoria there was some bitterness towards the Government after the people had heard news of Germany's unconditional surrender from German sources only. As each hours past, there was still no official announcement from the British Government as the mood of excitement changed to one of impatience.

As the *Evening Telegraph* put it: "Let's have news that it's VE Day and be done with it!"

In Derby Market Place, a Trent bus conductress, on hearing that the Germans had announced their surrender, proclaimed: "That's good enough for me. I've got a day off!" But a man nearby grumbled: "We've got it from every country in the world – except our own."

Some LMS workers decided not wait and downed tools. Company officials held a hasty meeting and decided to let the workers go, except for those doing essential work.

It was had been known for some days that the end was imminent and on 4 May the *Derby Evening Telegraph* had announced that on "VE Day Plus One" it would not publish.

Uncertain whether the holiday announcement applied to them, many workers turned up, only to be sent back home. Outside the Rolls-Royce factory in Nightingale Road, workers strolled in groups, discussing how to spend the rest of the day.

The confusion had arisen by a change in arrangements when, because VE Day itself had been announced so late, so the following day was also declared a holiday. Departmental heads at Rolls-Royce eventually decided that work should begin again with the night-shift on the Thursday.

At teatime on VE Day, the Harrison family of Middleton Street received a great surprise. Through the door, to the delight of his wife and family, came Corporal "Sid" Harrison of the RASC. Forty-

Residents of Harrington Street all set for their VE Day street party.

four-year-old Corporal Harrison had made his way home from a German PoW camp, where he had been since his capture in 1941.

Throughout the week the people of Derby had been seeing the first evidence of one of the most terrible episodes in European history as newsreels in cinemas across the town showed scenes recorded by army cameramen entering the concentration camps at Belsen and Buchenwald.

For the people of Derby, the Second World War had ended, in Europe at least, but it would be some time yet before the revellers could put their minds to turning victory over Hitler into a lasting peace. Many of them had husbands and sweethearts, sons and brothers, still fighting the Japanese in the jungles of the Far East.

It was not until the explosion of two nuclear bombs over the cities of Hiroshima and Nagasaki, three months later, that Japan surrendered . And even then it would be some months before the troops began to return home.

There were many happy homecomings, of course, but for many more the world would never be the same. Years of fighting or captivity, often in the most barbaric conditions, had changed them; and in different ways the war had also changed the ones they had left behind.

VJ Day – Victory over Japan – on 8 August, 1945, was about as confusing as VE Day. Most people assumed that the second victory holiday of the summer would not begin until the Thursday. So the majority did not hear the Prime Minister's midnight announcement and awoke uncertain as to whether this would be just another normal day. The result was that hundreds set off for work as usual and it was not until the victory peals were sounded by the bells of Derby Cathedral that they realised the war was finally over. Housewives rushed to town to queue for fish, meat, bread, and even flags. By 9.30am demand for bread was so great that bakers were restricting supplies to one loaf per customer.

There were angry scenes outside the Co-op's main store in East Street. It was closed and many of the women had not drawn their weekly rations of fat and other cooking requirements. A queue of 60 women waited for the Co-op offices in Albion to open so that they could draw their "divi", only to be told that the Co-op would be closed for two days.

Of 180 Corporation bus employees on the early shift, all but 50 turned up for work. Buses ran to take night shift workers home, and staff to the City and Isolation Hospitals, before the bus crews themselves were stood down for the rest of the day.

With two-day leave passes in their pockets, hundreds of servicemen and women head for the LMS Station, where queues for trains stretched down Midland Road as army and RAF personnel from bases around the town tried desperately to get home in time for the victory celebrations. There had been scenes of wild excitement in the early hours of the morning outside Normanton Barracks. The midnight broadcast had been the signal for merrymaking and ATS girls stationed there had donned overcoats over their nightclothes and spilled out of the depot to celebrate.

Members of the Sherwood Foresters Band drew their instruments and soon a dance was in full swing on the barrack square as hundreds of nearby residents came out of their houses to join in. The vicar of Normanton arrived and civilians and soldiers joined in a service at the gates to the barracks.

Men on night shift at the Carriage and Wagon Works heard of the surrender and decided to leave work for "a couple of hours of jollification". When official sanction was denied them, they simply dragged the canteen piano into one of the sheds and began a sing-song which lasted until dawn. And a truckload of black American troops made merry by "careering around the town centre shouting and singing".

On VJ Day, there were plenty of street parties. In Rivett Street, 30 children enjoyed home-made cakes and buns; the major feature of the party in Melbourne Street was a 7lbs iced "Victory Peace Cake" made by Mrs Ethel Wright; old age pensioners were invited to a children's party in King Alfred Street and enjoyed fruit, jelly, cakes and buns.

In Goodwin Street, 161 happy faces testified to the quality of the fare bought by the £9 5s collected for the occasion; children in Offerton Avenue burned an effigy of the Japanese warlord Togo;

the anti-aircraft battery on Kingsway loaned their canteen so that the children of the Westleigh Estate could stage their party.

And on Chester Green there was a football match between local men and women who swapped clothes for the occasion. At St James's Road School, the problem of finding enough fat to bake cakes was solved when Mrs H. Rawlings went round the neighbourhood to beg a piece of margarine "the size of a walnut" from each resident. Soon she had enough to begin work.

At midnight in the Market Place, a huge crowd sang *Abide With Me* before falling into a two-minute silence to remember the dead. Earlier, thousands had danced to the accompaniment of the Rolls-Royce Band, which competed with several impromptu "orchestras" around the square.

In December 1945, Jim Phelps, the nine-year-old boy we met at the beginning of this story of Derby's war, was now 16. On Christmas morning he went to Rosehill Methodist Church on Normanton Road where there were some German prisoners-of-war in the congregation.

They sat shoulder to shoulder with their fellow worshippers, some of the ordinary people of Derby, and together they sang *Silent Night*.

Jim said: "My mind went back to that September day when war was declared and I thought about all the horror, the hurt and heartache. And then I wondered what we had learned, and what tomorrow would bring."